Whoopie Pies

An Imagine Book
Published by Charlesbridge
85 Main Street, Watertown, MA 02472
617-926-0329
www.charlesbridge.com

Created by Penn Publishing Ltd.
1 Yehuda Halevi Street, Tel Aviv, Israel 65135
www.penn.co.il

Editor-in-Chief: Rachel Penn
Edited by Sebastia Richter
Design and layout by Michal & Dekel
Photography by Danya Weiner
Food styling by Deanna Linder

Library of Congress Cataloging-in-Publication Data

Goren, Viola.
 Whoopie pies / Viola Goren ; photography by Danya Weiner.
    p. cm. -- (An imagine book)
 Includes index.
 ISBN 978-1-936140-52-7
1. Whoopie pies. 2. Cookbooks. I. Weiner, Danya. II. Title.
 TX772.G66 2011
 641.8'652--dc22
                            2011015161

2 4 6 8 10 9 7 5 3 1

Printed in China, May 2011

For information about custom editions, special sales, premium and corporate purchases,
please contact Charlesbridge Publishing at specialsales@charlesbridge.com

Whoopie Pies

Viola Goren

Photography by
Danya Weiner

imagine!
Publishing

Contents

Introduction

The **"Whoopie Pie"** is the latest classic craze sweeping the culinary world. It is an old-fashioned treat-its roots were as a glorious Amish treat. Now it's making a nostalgic comeback in a fancier version. The Whoopie Pie will satisfy any craving for a handmade sweet to bring both comfort and delight, allowing you to reminisce about "the good old days" of handmade pastries and quality family time.

The Whoopie Pie, also referred to as "the new cupcake", is a small personal cake. It is essentially a mini-sandwich made from two soft cookies with a creamy filling in between. Known also as "gobs," the exact origin of this treat is a bit uncertain, though the states of Maine and Pennsylvania both claim this privilege.

Everything about the Whoopie Pie is intended for fun-even its name! According to Amish legend, Pennsylvanian women would bake the pies from leftover cake batter as a lunchtime dessert. When farmers and children opened their lunch boxes, they would find the treat and shout with delight, "Whoopie!" So will you!

Baked for less than ten minutes, the Whoopie Pie is quick and easy to prepare. These adorable goodies are perfect for any party, get-together or holiday, as well as a special post-lunch dessert. It is a celebration for the kids from start to finish: the creams, the colorful decorations and the topping variations are almost endless.

In this book I will offer home-bakers both inspiration and play tools, combined with well-chosen ingredients used to bake special Whoopie Pies. You can enjoy traditional flavors, as well as new tastes and combinations, inspired by international cuisine. My origins lie in the French kitchen, so I will mostly be combining French pastry sophistication with classic American tastes.

Many of the recipes in this book have their origins in Europe. For example, the Black Forest is actually of German origin, but takes on an American twist here. There is also a whole chapter dedicated to savory Whoopie Pies, packed with ideas to enhance flavor and enrich texture. Keep in mind that although the contemporary version of the Whoopie Pie fuses flavors like simple vanilla with ginger and coconut, the basic, easy-to-make recipe remains unchanged. From fruity to chocolaty to savory, all of your taste buds will reawaken with scintillating delight.

The recipes in this book can be used not only for baking Whoopie Pies, but also for normal-sized cakes and birthday cakes. In this case, you just bake the batter in a regular cake circle mold, douse it with multi-colored birthday sprinkles, light a few candles on the top and turn off the lights to make a wish!

Be creative, imaginative and experimental when baking! Before preparing the Whoopie Pie, read the recipe and try to feel the flavors on your tongue. Open your refrigerator and check out what materials you have, what can be added, what you might try or which combinations are possible. Additionally, you can check in this book for other recipes that include a flavor you desire. If you are out of a specific ingredient for the recipe, do not let this discourage you. Use your imagination and find a suitable alternative in your kitchen!

Finally, think and act like a professional baker on an assembly line: consider how you might simplify the work (pages 8 and 16, for example).

I hope that you and your loved ones will have lots of fun preparing and eating your own homemade Whoopie Pies.

Now get ready. Fasten your seatbelts and enjoy some Whoopie time travel!

Whoopie Pie Essentials

Secret tips and techniques, equipment and ingredients, decorating ideas and storage.

Avoid Overmixing

The Whoopie Pie is actually a miniature cake. Similar to pound cake, the Whoopie Pie is made from four basic ingredients: flour, butter, eggs and sugar. Thus, it is important that the batter stay compressed, compact and dense, rather than thin. Furthermore, avoid overmixing to ensure a round shape.

Baking Time

The time needed for cooking will depend on your oven. Check it often to make sure it does not overcool.

Cakes

- The baking process is one of trial and exploration. Every recipe consists of a basic structure, to which one adds spices and flavors. I recommend that you make creativity and playfulness a part of the process.
- Remember that spices are replaceable and interchangeable. Adjust according to your preference; you can add or omit ingredients, such as cinnamon, to suit your taste.
- Be sure to make a note of these alterations and amounts in the margins of the recipe, so you will remember your changes and successful additions in the future.
- When making Whoopie Pies, always start and end with flour.
- Add basic ingredients gradually, as follows:

1. Start with one third of the amount of flour called for in the recipe.

2. Then add half the amount of the sour cream or crème fraiche.

3. Next, add an additional third of the amount of flour, and then the second half of the sour cream.

4. Finally, add the last third of the flour and the dry ingredients.

- Be sure to add the next ingredient when the previous addition is almost, but not completely, mixed in. You need not wait until all of the flour is dissolved, for example. Add the sour cream once it is only partly mixed in. When some of the sour cream has been incorporated, add the rest of the ingredients.

Cooling

- All the batter ingredients must be cold.
- Never add hot ingredients to the batter. Allow them to cool first; otherwise, they will cause the batter to be runny and it will spread out.
- If any fruits or nuts require toasting, for example, set them aside to cool before mixing them in.

Grinding

- It is preferable to grind whole nuts yourself instead of buying prepared nut powder. Freshly-ground nuts retain their aroma better. Remember that nuts contain oil. Know when to stop grinding so as to avoid over-processing the powder into a purée.

- **Tip:** For recipes containing flour, you can add a bit of flour from the recipe. Grind the mass some more; the flour will absorb the oils and adjust the texture properly.

Sifting

- Sifting breaks up clumps and adds air to flour, resulting in a lighter Whoopie cake. Sifting also helps for uniform measure and equal blending of dry ingredients. I recommend preparing two separate bowls, one for dry and one for wet materials.
- Start by sifting together the flour, baking powder, baking soda, powdered sugar and cocoa powder. Be sure to sift the cocoa at the end. Although it is not a necessity, I suggest having a separate smaller sifter for the cocoa powder.
- Do not sift spices, as they are too granulated and may get stuck in the sifter.

Roasting Nuts

In recipes that call for nuts, I recommend that you roast them for a few minutes first. Begin by rinsing them under running water until all the nuts are wet. Shake off excess water and season with salt or other seasonings, according to taste. Spread the nuts, ideally with skins, on a baking sheet and toast in a warm oven for 7-10 minutes, or until the color changes slightly and the skins are blistered. When they have cooled, rub the nuts lightly between your fingers to remove the skins.

Equipment

Most of the tools necessary to make Whoopie Pies can be found in your average kitchen. Some more professional tools, such as thermometers and scales, are helpful and will serve you well in all baking and cooking adventures for years to come. It is worthwhile investing in good quality necessary tools. Start building your collection of baking tools piece by piece.

Basic Measuring Tools

The most accurate way to measure the amounts and quantities of the ingredients listed in the recipes is to use a weight measurement tool, such as a digital scale. Alternatively, you can use standard measurement tools, such as measuring cups, tablespoons and teaspoons. These tools are available at specialty stores.

Mixer With Paddle Attachment

Although all recipes in this book can be made by hand, baking is usually easier and cleaner with an electric mixer. I recommend using a standing mixer, not a handheld one. The stand mixer is more stable and comfortable to use. Be sure to use a flat beater with a paddle attachment.

Oven

It's important to familiarize yourself with your oven because each oven behaves a bit differently. Some have a temperature deviation of 20°F. Place the Whoopie Pies in the middle of the oven. Check on them throughout the baking process. To ensure even baking, rotate every now and then while the cake is baking. This prevents one side coming out burned, while the other is not completely baked through.

Pastry Bags (optional)

You can purchase pastry bags at any specialty cooking shop. They come with various tips as well. Alternately, you can easily make your own pastry bag at home. Fill an average-size zip-lock bag with the filling; use scissors to cut a small hole in the corner to pipe

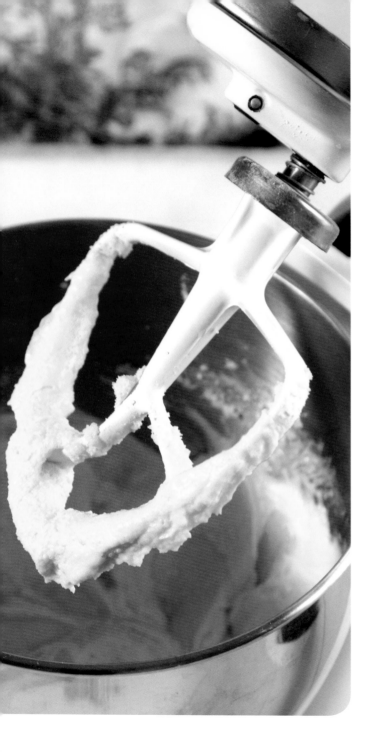

the fillings through. Of course, you can do without a pastry bag and spread the filling with a spoon or spatula. The problem with this is that it will be spread unevenly. If you prefer to preserve the round shape and have a smoother and elegant finish, a pastry bag is highly recommended.

Thermometer (optional)

The built-in temperature indicator in the oven is not always exact. (For example, the thermometer in the oven could show 180°F when the actual temperature is 200°F). I recommend buying a small oven thermometer and hanging it in the oven where you can see it easily. This will tell you the exact temperature of your oven.

Timer

Timing is crucial in baking; therefore, it is essential to have a good and accurate timer.

Wire Cooling Rack

- After baking, it is important to prevent steam from collecting on the bottoms of the Whoopie Pies while they are cooling. Otherwise, they turn damp and spongy. A wire cooling rack allows for faster cooling because air circulates all around the pies—the heat escapes and the moisture does not build up.
- Parchment paper is another solution. Handy and inexpensive, it is also ideal for baking.
- A third option, though more expensive, is a silicon mat. This tool can serve you well into the future.

Ingredients

Who doesn't have butter, eggs, flour and sugar in their refrigerator? Most, if not all, of these ingredients are in your kitchen at any point in time. No need to plan ahead or go on a special grocery shopping spree. Just take out the ingredients and start baking these satisfying, delightful, ready-to-bake treats!

Butter

Butter adds a creamy flavor and a rich taste to any recipe. It is best to use unsalted butter at room temperature. If you use cold butter, you will require a longer baking time.

Eggs

Use fresh medium-size eggs at room temperature. It is best to add the yolk first and then egg white. 'Fish' the yolks out by hand, rather than separating the white from the cracked egg.

Tip: If you break the eggs instead of separating them, use refrigerated eggs.

Flour

- Most of the recipes in the book call for all-purpose flour.
  To measure flour properly, pour it into a jar or measuring cup so that there is a slight overflow. Use a knife to lever off the top so that the exact amount of flour is left. Flour should be kept in a cool, dry cupboard.
- Some of the recipes call for healthier flour substitutes, such as corn flour or gluten-free flour. These serve as substitutes for people who are sensitive to gluten or who keep kosher during the Jewish holiday of Passover.

Food Coloring

- Food coloring is not necessary, but it can be fun. It is difficult to know the exact quantity to add, as some colors are stronger than others. Add coloring slowly to achieve the desired color.
- For softer pastel colors, use very little color, especially with frosting.
- Remember that the process is irreversible unless you prepare more dough and combine the two together.

Heavy Cream

Also called whipping cream, heavy cream should always be stored in the refrigerator. Only very cold cream whips properly.

Salt

Although it may seem an odd addition to sweet dishes, a touch of salt actually accentuates flavors.

Sugar

Use granulated sugar for all recipes unless another type, such as brown or powdered sugar, is specifically mentioned. Sugar should be stored in a tightly sealed container in a cool, dry cupboard.

Decorating Ideas

Traditional Whoopie Pies are usually not decorated. Once assembled, however, it can be fun to enhance the tops with the decorations and toppings you desire. Be creative and choose from old favorites or more unusual ones.

Tip: Allow the Whoopie Pies to cool and set before decorating, piping or spreading the filling. Keep in mind that sprinkles will not stick to ready-baked cookies unless you frost them first. Therefore, it is important to spread the sprinkles before baking to ensure them from sliding off.

Dipping

You can dip the assembled Whoopie Pie in few ways:

- Half dipping

Dip half of each assembled cookie from the side in melted semisweet chocolate or ganâche. This will add a hard coating. Once dipped, you can roll it in any coating of your liking. Be sure to allow the Whoopie Pies to cool and the chocolate to set.

Tip: If you have made a batch of chocolate ganâche, keep it in the fridge until firm.

- Two color dipping

You can prepare both white and dark chocolate (either ganâche or regular) and dip each half of the Whoopie Pie into a different color to create a black and white effect.

Rolling

Press and roll the edges of each cooled cookie into cocoa powder, sprinkles, shredded or crushed candies, nuts or halva, shredded coconut, poppy seeds, chocolate shavings or any other coatings.

Sprinkling

To add a delectably pretty finish to the tops of the Whoopie Pie, sprinkle cocoa powder, multi-colored sprinkles of any kind, poppy seeds, confectioners' sugar, cinnamon or anything else that takes your fancy.

Topping

You can serve the Whoopie Pie plain or top it with a scoop of your favorite ice cream.

Storage Suggestions

Whoopie Pies taste best when they are fresh and slightly cooled. You can store Whoopie Pies in an airtight container in the refrigerator for up to a week. Whoopie Pies can also be stored in the freezer for a few months. Allow them to thaw in the refrigerator. I personally don't recommend reheating Whoopie Pies.

Storing Creams

You can store buttercream in an airtight container in the refrigerator for up to 2-3 weeks; similarly, ganâche chocolate lasts for up to three months. Cheese fillings only last a week or less, depending on the type of cheese and the expiration date. Use the extra fillings and toppings for your next batch of Whoopie Pies.

Recipes

The Creamy Fillings

French Buttercream Filling

Makes filling for 20 - 25

People who are allergic to dairy products can use butter-flavored margarine instead of butter. To reduce the buttery flavor, add an extra tablespoon of vanilla extract or zest of lemon or orange.

Ingredients

- 4 egg whites
- 1 cup sugar
- 1 teaspoon vanilla extract
- 8 oz butter at room temperature, cut into small cubes

Preparation

1. Pour egg whites and sugar into a bowl placed over a pot of hot water (double boiler). Stir constantly until sugar is dissolved.

2. Beat eggs until mixture cools. Then gradually add vanilla extract and butter. Mix until cream is smooth and uniform.

French Buttercream Filling

Classic Marshmallow Cream

Makes filling for 20 - 25

I like to store the vanilla stick in the sugar to make vanilla sugar.
To prepare vanilla powder, take a few vanilla beans and put them in the oven briefly to dry them out until they crumble easily. Let them cool before grinding them. For a more intense flavor in a vanilla Whoopie Pie, add beans scraped from a vanilla stick.

Ingredients

- 8 ounces butter, at room temperature
- 1 cup powdered sugar
- ½ vanilla stick
- 1½ cups marshmallow fluff

Preparation

- **1.** Cream butter, powdered sugar and scraped out vanilla beans in an electric mixer with a flat beater for about 5 minutes, until the mixture is light and airy.

- **2.** Add marshmallow fluff and continue beating the mixture, until the mixture has a uniform consistency.

Maple Cream

Makes filling for 20 - 25

For variety, try replacing the maple syrup with honey or silan (date honey).

Ingredients

- 8 ounces soft cream cheese
- 1 cup powdered sugar
- 1 tablespoon heavy whipping cream
- 2 tablespoons maple syrup

Preparation

- **1.** In a separate bowl, mix cream cheese and powdered sugar with the mixer's flat beater, until the mixture is light and airy.

- **2.** Add whipping cream and maple syrup, scraping the sides of the bowl as needed. Mix well until the batter is uniform.

Meringue Cream

You can freeze the yolks until needed.
Be sure to thaw in the refrigerator.

Ingredients

- 4 egg whites
- 1 cup sugar

Preparation

- **1.** Pour egg whites and sugar into a bowl placed over a pot of hot water (double boiler). Stir constantly until sugar is dissolved.

- **2.** Transfer to mixing bowl and beat on medium speed, then on high speed, until the mixture cools completely and the meringue is set.

Lemon Mascarpone Cream

You can use raspberry, blackberry or strawberry jam instead of orange zest and lemon juice.

Ingredients

- 1½ cups powdered sugar
- 4 ounces mascarpone cheese
- Zest of 1 lemon
- 1 teaspoon lemon juice

Preparation

- **1.** In a bowl, sift powdered sugar.

- **2.** Place mascarpone cheese and powdered sugar in a mixing bowl. Beat with the mixer's flat beater. Then add lemon zest and lemon juice.

- **3.** Mix well until mixture is smooth and airy.

Dulce de Leche Cream

Makes filling for 20 - 25

The cream can be kept in a sealed container in the refrigerator for up to 4 days. Before using, stir well using a whisk, until a smooth consistency is achieved.

I usually freeze the egg whites and use them when I need them. Frozen egg whites can keep for up to a week. Be sure to thaw in the refrigerator before using.

Ingredients

- 1 cup milk
- 1 teaspoon vanilla extract
- ½ cup sugar
- 4 egg yolks
- 2 tablespoons cornstarch
- 1 tablespoon flour
- ½ cup Dulce de Leche paste

Preparation

1. In a saucepan, heat milk and vanilla extract just to boiling. Remove from heat.

2. In a bowl, whisk sugar and egg yolks. Gradually add cornstarch and flour. Mix well until mixture is uniform.

3. Pour ⅓ of the milk mixture into the bowl, while constantly stirring.

4. Heat remaining milk mixture over a low heat, add egg mixture and stir constantly. Cook until cream firms and thickens.

5. Remove from heat and stir.

6. Add Dulce de Leche paste and mix.

7. Press a piece of plastic wrap against the surface to create an airtight seal and then refrigerate.

Mocha Cream

Makes filling for 20 - 25

You can use coffee extract, found at specialty stores, or alternatively substitute with coffee liqueur.

You can also melt the chocolate in the microwave. Be sure to run the microwave in 20-30 second increments.

Ingredients

- 4 egg whites
- 1 cup sugar
- 1 teaspoon vanilla extract
- 8 oz butter at room temperature, cut into cubes
- 2 tablespoons instant coffee powder +
  1 tablespoon boiling water
- 4 ounces dark chocolate, coarsely chopped

Preparation

1. Pour egg whites and sugar into a bowl and place over a pot of hot water (double boiler). Stir constantly until sugar is dissolved.

2. Beat the egg whites until the mixture cools.

3. Gradually add vanilla extract and butter.

4. Dissolve instant coffee powder in boiling water.

5. Pour chocolate into a bowl and place over a pot of hot water (double boiler), stirring constantly until chocolate is melted. Avoid all contact with water - even a few droplets. (Otherwise the chocolate will separate and become unusable.)

6. Add chocolate mixture and instant coffee (prepared in Step 4) to cream and stir well, until cream is smooth.

Mocha Cream

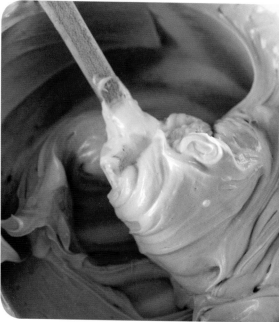

Chocolate Hazelnut (Nutella) Cream

Chocolate Hazelnut (Nutella) Cream

Makes filling for 20 - 25

If wrapped well, this cream can be stored in the refrigerator for up to a week.

Ingredients

- 4 egg whites
- 1 cup sugar
- 3 ounces butter at room temperature, cut into cubes
- ½ cup Nutella spread

Preparation

1. Pour egg whites and sugar into a bowl placed over a pot of hot water (double boiler). Stir constantly until sugar is dissolved.

2. Transfer to mixing bowl and beat on medium speed, then on high speed, until mixture cools completely and the meringue is set.

3. Gradually add butter and Nutella spread.

4. Mix well until the cream is smooth and uniform.

Tiramisu, Mascarpone Cheese & Coffee Cream

Makes filling for 20 - 25

You can use coffee liqueur instead of coffee extract.

Ingredients

- 2 oz butter, at room temperature
- 4 ounces mascarpone cheese
- 1½ cups powdered sugar
- 1 tablespoon coffee extract (or 1 teaspoon instant coffee powder, dissolved in water)

Preparation

1. Cream butter, mascarpone cheese, powdered sugar and coffee extract in an electric mixer with a flat beater, until mixture is uniform.

Chocolate Buttercream Filling

Makes filling for 20 - 25

For chocolate lovers who need to satisfy their intense craving for chocolate, add an extra 6 ounces of milk chocolate or 8 ounces of white chocolate. These options provide a richer flavor and extra-velvety texture.

Ingredients

- 4 ounces dark chocolate, coarsely chopped
- 4 egg yolks
- 1 cup sugar
- 1 teaspoon vanilla extract
- 8 oz butter at room temperature, cut into small cubes

Preparation

- **1.** In a bowl placed over a pot of hot water (double boiler), melt chocolate and mix until smooth. Remove from heat and cool.

- **2.** Pour yolks and sugar into a bowl placed over a pot of hot water (double boiler). Stir constantly until sugar is dissolved. Beat eggs until mixture cools.

- **3.** Gradually add vanilla extract and butter.

- **4.** Pour in melted chocolate and mix well, until cream is smooth and uniform.

Chocolate Buttercream Filling

Goat
Cheese
Cream

Makes filling for 20 - 25

For variety, replace the goat cheese with ricotta cheese.

Ingredients

- 1 cup goat cheese
- 3-4 tablespoons heavy whipping cream

Preparation

1. Cream goat cheese and whipping cream in an electric mixer with flat beater, until mixture is light and airy.

Milk
Chocolate
Ganâche

Makes filling for 20 - 25

This scrumptious chocolate ganâche has many uses. In its liquid state, it can be poured over a cake as a glaze. Allow the ganâche to cool slightly before pouring.

Ingredients

- 1 cup heavy whipping cream
- 15 ounces milk chocolate, coarsely chopped
- 3 ounces butter, at room temperature

Preparation

1. In a small saucepan, bring whipping cream just to a boil. Then remove from heat.

2. Add chopped chocolate and butter.

3. Wait about 1 minute until chocolate melts. Then, using a whisk, mix cream and chocolate in the center of the bowl, until the consistency is smooth. Set aside to cool before using.

Cream Cheese Filling

Makes filling for 20 - 25

For variety, use mascarpone or ricotta cheese.

Ingredients

- 8 ounces cream cheese
- 1 cup powdered sugar
- 1 tablespoon heavy whipping cream
- 1 teaspoon lemon or orange juice

Preparation

1. Mix cream cheese and powdered sugar in an electric mixer with a flat beater, until mixture is light and airy.

2. Add whipping cream and lemon or orange juice, scraping sides of bowl as needed. Continue beating until mixture has a uniform consistency.

Savory Cream Cheese Filling

Makes filling for 20 - 25

You can replace the cream cheese with any other soft white cheese. Make sure the excess liquid has been drained first.

Ingredients

- 1 cup cream cheese
- 2 tablespoons heavy whipping cream

Preparation

1. Beat cream cheese with whipping cream in an electric mixer with a flat beater, until mixture is light and airy.

Dark Chocolate Ganâche

Makes filling for 20 - 25

I like to prepare a double batch of the ganâche and use the leftover filling to make truffles. Simply refrigerate the ganâche and then roll it into small balls. Coat each truffle ball with cocoa powder, coconut or ground nuts.

Ingredients

- 1 cup heavy whipping cream
- 10 ounces dark chocolate, coarsely chopped
- 2 ounces butter, at room temperature

Preparation

- **1.** In a small saucepan, bring whipping cream just to a boil. Then remove from heat.

- **2.** Add chopped chocolate and butter.

- **3.** Wait about 1 minute until chocolate melts. Then, using a whisk, mix cream and chocolate in the center of the bowl, until the consistency is smooth.

- **4.** Set aside to cool before using.

Dark Chocolate Ganâche

White Chocolate Ganâche

Makes filling for 20 - 25

This recipe can be made with or without butter. Butter adds firmness and enriches the cream.

Ingredients

- 1 cup heavy whipping cream
- 18 oz white chocolate, coarsely chopped
- 4 oz butter, at room temperature

Preparation

- *1.* In a small saucepan, bring whipping cream just to a boil. Then remove from heat.

- *2.* Add chopped chocolate and butter.

- *3.* Wait about 1 minute until chocolate melts. Then, using a whisk, mix cream and chocolate in the center of the bowl, until the consistency is smooth.

- *4.* Set aside to cool before using.

White Chocolate Ganâche

Fruit Delights

Cherry Whoopie Pie

I like to mix cherries into the batter before baking as well as into the cream before assembling.

In this recipe you can use fresh, frozen or canned cherries.

Ingredients

- 2 cups flour
- 1½ teaspoons baking powder
- ⅓ cup shredded coconut
- 4 ounces butter, at room temperature
- 1⅓ cups sugar
- 2 eggs
- ½ cup crème fraiche
- ¾ cup cherries, halved and pitted, cut into small pieces

French Buttercream Filling

- 4 egg whites
- 1 cup sugar
- 1 teaspoon vanilla extract
- 8 oz butter at room temperature, cut into small cubes

Makes 20 - 25

Preparation

1. Preheat the oven to 350°F.

2. Line baking sheets with parchment paper or use silicone baking mats.

3. **Prepare cakes:** In a bowl, using a rubber spatula, mix flour, baking powder and shredded coconut.

4. Place butter and sugar in a separate mixing bowl. Beat with the electric mixer's flat beater, until mixture is light and airy. Then add eggs,one at a time, mixing well.

5. Gradually add the dry ingredients (prepared in Step 3), crème fraiche and cherries. Mix until incorporated.

6. Drop batter onto prepared baking sheets, spacing evenly. Spread batter into approximately 1¼-inch circles.

7. Bake for 7-10 minutes or until cakes are springy to the touch and a toothpick, inserted in center of a cake, comes out clean.

8. Remove from oven and allow to cool completely on a wire rack.

9. **Prepare filling:** Pour egg whites and sugar into a bowl placed over a pot of hot water (double boiler). Stir constantly until sugar is dissolved.

10. Beat eggs until mixture cools. Then gradually add vanilla extract and butter. Mix until cream is smooth and uniform.

11. When the cakes are completely cool, spread filling onto the flat side of a cake and top it with another cake. Press gently on top until filling spreads to edges.

Cherry Whoopie Pie

Blueberry Whoopie Pie

You can use fresh, frozen or canned blueberries. If you use the latter, drain the berries from the preserving juice first.

Ingredients

- 2 cups flour
- ½ cup almond flour
- 1½ teaspoons baking powder
- 4 oz butter, at room temperature
- 1⅓ cups sugar
- Zest of 1 lemon
- 2 eggs
- ½ cup crème fraiche
- ¾ cup blueberries, fresh or frozen

French Buttercream Filling

- 4 egg whites
- 1 cup sugar
- 1 teaspoon vanilla extract
- 8 oz butter at room temperature, cut into small cubes

Makes 20 - 25

Preparation

1. Preheat the oven to 350°F.

2. Line baking sheets with parchment paper or use silicone baking mats.

3. Prepare cakes: In a bowl, using a rubber spatula, mix flour, almond flour and baking powder.

4. Place butter, sugar and zest of lemon in a separate mixing bowl. Beat with the mixer's flat beater until mixture is light and airy. Then add eggs, one at a time, mixing well.

5. Gradually add dry ingredients (prepared in Step 3), crème fraiche and blueberries. Mix until incorporated.

6. Drop batter onto prepared baking sheets, spacing evenly. Spread batter into approximately 1¼-inch circles.

7. Bake for 7-10 minutes or until cakes are springy to the touch and a toothpick, inserted in center of a cake, comes out clean.

8. Remove from oven and allow to cool completely on a wire rack.

9. Prepare filling: Pour egg whites and sugar into a bowl placed over a pot of hot water (double boiler). Stir constantly until sugar is dissolved.

10. Beat eggs until mixture cools. Then gradually add vanilla extract and butter. Mix until cream is smooth and uniform.

11. When the cakes are completely cool, spread filling onto the flat side of a cake and top it with another cake. Press gently on top until filling spreads to edges.

Blueberry Whoopie Pie

Raspberry Whoopie Pie

I love adding raspberries into the filling, these introduce color and texture.

Ingredients

- 2⅓ cups flour
- 1½ teaspoons baking powder
- 4 oz butter, at room temperature
- ¾ cup sugar
- ½ cup brown sugar
- Zest of 1 lemon
- 2 eggs
- ½ cup crème fraiche
- ¾ cup fresh or frozen raspberries

French Buttercream Filling

- 4 egg whites
- 1 cup sugar
- 1 teaspoon vanilla extract
- 8 oz butter at room temperature, cut into small cubes

Makes 20 - 25

Preparation

1. Preheat the oven to 350°F.

2. Line baking sheets with parchment paper or use silicone baking mats.

3. **Prepare cakes:** In a bowl, using a rubber spatula, mix flour and baking powder.

4. Place butter, sugars and zest of lemon in a separate mixing bowl, beating with the mixer's flat beater until mixture is light and airy. Then add eggs, one at a time, mixing well.

5. Gradually add dry ingredients (prepared in Step 3), crème fraiche and raspberries. Mix until incorporated.

6. Drop batter onto prepared baking sheets, spacing evenly. Spread batter into approximately 1¼-inch circles.

7. Bake for 7-10 minutes or until cakes are springy to the touch and a toothpick, inserted in center of a cake, comes out clean.

8. Remove from oven and allow to cool completely on a wire rack.

9. **Prepare filling:** Pour egg whites and sugar into a bowl placed over a pot of hot water (double boiler). Stir constantly until sugar is dissolved.

10. Beat eggs until mixture cools. Then gradually add vanilla extract and butter. Mix until cream is smooth and uniform.

11. When the cakes are completely cool, spread filling onto the flat side of a cake and top it with another cake. Press gently on top until filling spreads to edges.

Apple with White Chocolate Whoopie Pie

For an elegant touch, you can top this Whoopie Pie with grated chocolate or chocolate strips, made with a vegetable peeler.

Makes 20 - 25

Ingredients

- 2 cups flour
- 2 teaspoons baking powder
- 1 teaspoon ground cinnamon
- ¼ teaspoon ground cloves
- 4 oz butter, at room temperature
- 1¾ cups sugar
- ½ cup brown sugar
- 2 eggs
- ⅓ cup crème fraiche
- 1 apple, shredded or thinly sliced
- ½ cup white chocolate chips

White Chocolate Ganâche

- 1 cup heavy whipping cream
- 18 oz white chocolate, coarsely chopped
- 4 oz butter, at room temperature

Preparation

1. Preheat the oven to 350°F.

2. Line baking sheets with parchment paper or use silicone baking mats.

3. Prepare cakes: In a bowl, using a rubber spatula, mix flour, baking powder, ground cinnamon and ground cloves.

4. Place butter and sugars in a separate mixing bowl, beating with the mixer's flat beater until mixture is light and airy. Then add eggs, one at a time, mixing well.

5. Gradually add dry ingredients (prepared in Step 3), crème fraiche, shredded apple and chocolate chips. Mix until incorporated.

6. Drop batter onto prepared baking sheets, spacing evenly. Spread batter into approximately 1¼-inch circles.

7. Bake for 7-10 minutes or until cakes are springy to the touch and a toothpick, inserted in the center of a cake, comes out clean. Remove from oven and allow to cool completely on a wire rack.

8. Prepare filling: In a small saucepan, bring whipping cream just to a boil. Then remove from heat. Add chopped chocolate and butter.

9. Wait about 1 minute until chocolate melts. Then, using a whisk, mix cream and chocolate in the center of the bowl until the ganâche has a smooth consistency.

10. Set aside to cool before using. When the cakes are completely cool, spread filling onto the flat side of a cake and top it with another cake. Press gently on top until filling spreads to edges.

Cinnamon Raisin Whoopie Pie

Cinnamon Raisin Whoopie Pie

You'll just love this Whoopie Pie. Your home will be filled with the warm and inviting scent of cinnamon, sugar and maple. It has a great balance of cinnamon and raisins; perfect for a morning snack. To enhance the flavor, I love adding zest of 1 lemon with the cinnamon.

Ingredients

- 2 cups flour
- 1 teaspoon baking powder
- 1 teaspoon baking soda
- 1 teaspoon lemon juice
- 1½ teaspoons ground cinnamon
- 4 ounces butter, at room temperature
- 1¼ cups sugar
- 2 teaspoons vanilla extract or ½ vanilla stick
- 2 eggs
- ½ cup sour cream
- 2 tablespoons heavy whipping cream
- ½ cup white raisins

Maple Cream

- 8 ounces soft cream cheese
- 1 cup powdered sugar
- 1 tablespoon heavy whipping cream
- 2 tablespoons maple syrup

Preparation

1. Preheat the oven to 350°F. Line baking sheets with parchment paper or use silicone baking mats.

2. Prepare cakes: In a bowl, using a rubber spatula, mix flour, baking powder and lemon juice.

3. Add ground cinnamon to mixture. Mix until incorporated.

4. Place butter, sugar and vanilla extract (or scraped out vanilla beans), in a separate mixing bowl and beat with the mixer's flat beater until mixture is light and airy. Then add eggs, one at a time, mixing well.

5. Gradually add dry ingredients mixture (prepared in Step 2), sour cream, whipping cream and raisins. Mix until incorporated.

6. Drop batter onto prepared baking sheets, spacing evenly. Spread batter into approximately 1¼-inch circles.

7. Bake for 7-10 minutes or until cakes are springy to the touch and a toothpick, inserted in center of a cake, comes out clean.

8. Remove from oven and allow to cool completely on a wire rack.

9. Prepare filling: In a separate bowl, mix cream cheese and powdered sugar with the mixer's flat beater until mixture is light and airy. Add whipping cream and maple syrup (scraping sides of bowl as needed). Mix well until the batter is uniform.

10. When the cakes are completely cool, spread filling onto the flat side of a cake and top it with another cake. Press gently on top until filling spreads to edges.

Lemon Whoopie Pie

For variety, replace the almond flour with shredded coconut, poppy seeds, pecans, walnuts or any other nuts. I recommend grinding your own roasted nuts (page 10).

Ingredients

- 2 cups flour
- ½ cup almond flour
- 1½ teaspoons baking powder
- 4 oz butter, at room temperature
- 1⅓ cups sugar
- Zest of 2 lemons
- 2 eggs
- ½ cup crème fraiche
- 1 tablespoon Limoncello

Lemon Mascarpone Cream

- 4 ounces mascarpone cheese
- ½ cup powdered sugar
- Zest of 1 lemon
- 1 teaspoon lemon juice

Makes 20 - 25

Preparation

1. Preheat the oven to 350°F.

2. Line baking sheets with parchment paper or use silicone baking mats.

3. Prepare cakes: In a bowl, using a rubber spatula, mix flour, almond flour and baking powder.

4. Place butter, sugar and lemon zest in a separate mixing bowl. Beat with the mixer's flat beater until mixture is light and airy. Then add eggs, one at a time, mixing well.

5. Gradually add dry ingredients (prepared in Step 3), crème fraiche and Limoncello. Mix until incorporated.

6. Drop batter onto prepared baking sheets, spacing evenly. Spread batter into approximately 1¼-inch circles.

7. Bake for 7-10 minutes or until cakes are springy to the touch and a toothpick, inserted in center of a cake, comes out clean.

8. Remove from oven and allow to cool completely on a wire rack.

9. Prepare filling: In a bowl, sift powdered sugar.

10. Place mascarpone cheese and powdered sugar in a mixing bowl, beating with the mixer's flat beater until evenly combined. Then add lemon zest and lemon juice. Mix well until mixture is smooth and airy.

11. When the cakes are completely cool, spread filling onto the flat side of a cake and top it with another cake. Press gently on top until filling spreads to edges.

Lemon Whoopie Pie

Orange-Lemon with Maple Cream Whoopie Pie

In any recipe that calls for orange or lemon zest, you can replace the zest with orange jam, or use thinly sliced dried oranges or lemons.

You can also replace the Maple Cream with Lemon Mascarpone Cream (page 24).

Ingredients

- 1¾ cups flour
- 2 teaspoons baking powder
- ½ cup ground blanched almonds
- 4 oz butter, at room temperature
- 1¼ cups sugar
- Zest of 1 orange
- Zest of 1 lemon
- 2 eggs
- ½ cup crème fraiche
- 1 tablespoon lemon juice

Maple Cream

- 8 oz soft cream cheese
- 1 cup powdered sugar
- 1 tablespoon heavy whipping cream
- 2 tablespoons maple syrup

Makes 20 - 25

Preparation

1. Preheat the oven to 350°F.

2. Line baking sheets with parchment paper or use silicone baking mats.

3. Prepare cakes: In a bowl, using a rubber spatula, mix flour, baking powder and ground almonds.

4. Place butter, sugar, zest of orange and zest of lemon in a separate mixing bowl. Beat with the mixer's flat beater, until mixture is light and airy. Then add eggs, one at a time, mixing well.

5. Gradually add dry ingredients (prepared in Step 3), crème fraiche and lemon juice. Mix until incorporated.

6. Drop batter onto prepared baking sheets, spacing evenly. Spread batter into approximately 1¼-inch circles.

7. Bake for 7-10 minutes or until cakes are springy to the touch and a toothpick, inserted in the center of a cake, comes out clean.

8. Remove from oven and allow to cool on a wire rack.

9. Prepare filling: In a separate bowl, mix cream cheese and powdered sugar with the mixer's flat beater until mixture is light and airy. Add whipping cream and maple syrup (scraping sides of bowl as needed). Mix until the batter is uniform.

10. When the cakes are completely cool, spread filling onto the flat side of a cake and top it with another cake. Press gently on top until filling spreads to edges.

Pistachio Marzipan & Cherry Whoopie Pie

Makes 20 - 25

Amarena cherries are expensive imports and may not be available in all grocery stores. Any other kind of cherry can be used, as well as canned cherries, drained of their preserving juice. Experiment by replacing the pistachios with almonds, poppy seeds or any other nuts.

Ingredients

- 1¾ cups flour
- 2 teaspoons baking powder
- ½ cup pistachios, finely grounded
- 4 oz butter, at room temperature
- 1¼ cups sugar
- 2 eggs
- ½ cup crème fraiche
- 2 oz marzipan, cut into cubes
- 3 oz Amarena cherries, pitted and thinly sliced

Cream Cheese Filling

- 8 oz cream cheese
- 1 cup powdered sugar
- 1 tablespoon heavy whipping cream
- 1 teaspoon lemon or orange juice

Preparation

1. Preheat the oven to 350°F.

2. Line baking sheets with parchment paper or use silicone baking mats.

3. **Prepare cakes:** In a bowl, using a rubber spatula, mix flour, baking powder and ground pistachios.

4. Place butter and sugar in a separate mixing bowl. Beat with the mixer's flat beater, until mixture is light and airy. Then add eggs, one at a time, mixing well.

5. Gradually add dry ingredients (prepared in Step 3), crème fraiche, marzipan cubes and cherries. Mix until incorporated.

6. Drop batter onto prepared baking sheets, spacing evenly. Spread batter into approximately 1¼-inch circles.

7. Bake for 7-10 minutes or until cakes are springy to the touch and a toothpick, inserted in the center of a cake, comes out clean.

8. Remove from oven and allow to cool completely on a wire rack.

9. **Prepare filling:** Mix cream cheese and powdered sugar in an electric mixer with a flat beater, until mixture is light and airy.

10. Add whipping cream and lemon or orange juice, scraping sides of bowl as needed. Continue beating until a uniform consistency is achieved.

11. When the cakes are completely cool, spread filling onto the flat side of a cake and top it with another cake. Press gently on top until filling spreads to edges.

Apple & Calvados Whoopie Pie

Apple & Calvados Whoopie Pie

For a special dinner party, surprise your guests with a unique flavor by using pears instead of apples.

Ingredients

- 2 cups flour
- 2 teaspoons baking powder
- 1 teaspoon ground cinnamon
- ¼ teaspoon ground cloves
- 4 oz butter, at room temperature
- 1¼ cups brown sugar
- 2 eggs
- ⅓ tablespoon crème fraiche
- 1 apple, shredded or thinly sliced
- 2 tablespoons Calvados

Maple Cream

- 8 ounces soft cream cheese
- 1 cup powdered sugar
- 1 tablespoon heavy whipping cream
- 2 tablespoons maple syrup

Makes 20 - 25

Preparation

1. Preheat the oven to 350°F.

2. Line baking sheets with parchment paper or use silicone baking mats.

3. Prepare cakes: In a bowl, using a rubber spatula, mix flour, baking powder, ground cinnamon and ground cloves.

4. Place butter and sugar in a separate mixing bowl, beating with the mixer's flat beater until mixture is light and airy. Then add eggs, one at a time, mixing well.

5. Gradually add dry ingredients (prepared in Step 3), crème fraiche, shredded apple and Calvados. Mix until incorporated.

6. Drop batter onto prepared baking sheets, spacing evenly. Spread batter into approximately 1¼-inch circles.

7. Bake for 7-10 minutes or until cakes are springy to the touch and a toothpick, inserted in the center of a cake, comes out clean.

8. Remove from oven and allow to cool completely on a wire rack.

9. Prepare filling: In a separate bowl, mix cream cheese and powdered sugar with the mixer's flat beater until mixture is light and airy. Add whipping cream and maple syrup (scraping sides of bowl as needed). Mix until the batter is uniform.

10. When the cakes are completely cool, spread filling onto the flat side of a cake and top it with another cake. Press gently on top until filling spreads to edges.

Candied Orange Whoopie Pie

Candied Orange Whoopie Pie

To make homemade candied orange: Preheat the oven to 280°F. Line the baking sheets with parchment paper. Cut 2 oranges (with the flesh) into slices. Place these in a saucepan with water and bring to a boil, simmer for 1 minute. Drain the water and repeat the process. Next, add 2 cups water and 2 cups sugar and bring to a boil again. Add the orange slices and cook for 15 minutes. Drain oranges peels. Transfer to the baking sheets and bake for 30 minutes. Remove from oven and set aside to cool.

Ingredients

- 1¾ cups flour
- 2 teaspoons baking powder
- 1½ cups ground blanched almonds
- 4 oz butter, at room temperature
- 1¼ cups sugar
- Zest of 1 orange
- 2 eggs
- ½ cup crème fraiche
- 1 tablespoon orange juice
- ½ cup candied orange, cut into cubes

Cream Cheese Filling

- 8 ounces cream cheese
- 1 cup powdered sugar
- 1 tablespoon heavy whipping cream
- 1 teaspoon lemon or orange juice

Preparation

1. Preheat the oven to 350°F.

2. Line baking sheets with parchment paper or use silicone baking mats.

3. Prepare cakes: In a bowl, using a rubber spatula, mix flour, baking powder and ground almonds.

4. Place butter, sugar and zest of orange in a separate mixing bowl, beating with the mixer's flat beater until mixture is light and airy. Then add eggs, one at a time, mixing well.

5. Gradually add dry ingredients (prepared in Step 3), crème fraiche, orange juice and candied orange. Mix until incorporated.

6. Drop batter onto prepared baking sheets, spacing evenly. Spread batter into approximately 1¼-inch circles.

7. Bake for 7-10 minutes or until cakes are springy to the touch and a toothpick, inserted in the center of a cake, comes out clean.

8. Remove from oven and allow to cool completely on a wire rack.

9. Prepare filling: Beat cream cheese and powdered sugar with the mixer's flat beater, until mixture is light and airy.

10. Add whipping cream and lemon or orange juice, scraping sides of bowl as needed. Continue beating until mixture has a uniform consistency.

11. When the cakes are completely cool, spread filling onto the flat side of a cake and top it with another cake. Press gently on top until filling spreads to edges.

Dried Apricot Whoopie Pie

For variety, you can replace the dried apricots with any other dried fruit.

Ingredients

- 1¾ cups flour
- 2 teaspoons baking powder
- ½ cup ground blanched almonds
- 4 oz butter, at room temperature
- 1¼ cups sugar
- 2 eggs
- ½ cup sour cream
- 4 oz dried apricots, cut into small cubes

Lemon Mascarpone Cream

- 4 oz mascarpone cheese
- 1½ cups powdered sugar
- Zest of 1 lemon
- 1 teaspoon lemon juice

Makes 20 - 25

Preparation

1. Preheat the oven to 350°F.

2. Line baking sheets with parchment paper or use silicone baking mats.

3. **Prepare cakes:** In a bowl, using a rubber spatula, mix flour, baking powder and ground almonds.

4. Place butter and sugar in a separate mixing bowl, beating with the mixer's flat beater, until mixture is light and airy. Then add eggs, one at a time, mixing well.

5. Gradually add dry ingredients (prepared in Step 3), sour cream and dried apricots. Mix until incorporated.

6. Drop batter onto prepared baking sheets, spacing evenly. Spread batter into approximately 1¼-inch circles.

7. Bake for 7-10 minutes or until cakes are springy to the touch and a toothpick, inserted in the center of a cake, comes out clean.

8. Remove from oven and allow to cool completely on a wire rack.

9. **Prepare filling:** Place mascarpone cheese and powdered sugar in a mixing bowl. Beat with the mixer's flat beater. Then add lemon zest and lemon juice. Mix well until mixture is smooth and airy.

10. When the cakes are completely cool, spread filling onto the flat side of a cake and top it with another cake. Press gently on top until filling spreads to edges.

Dried Apricot Whoopie Pie

Hawaiian Pineapple Coconut Whoopie Pie

Canned pineapple is tastier than fresh one because it is sweeter. If you use fresh pineapple in season and it is not quite sweet enough, add a ¼ cup of sugar.

Ingredients

- 1¾ cups flour
- 2 teaspoons baking powder
- ⅓ cup shredded coconut
- 4 oz butter, at room temperature
- 1¼ cups sugar
- 2 eggs
- ½ cup sour cream
- ½ cup pineapple, fresh or canned, cut into small cubes

Maple Cream

- 8 ounces soft cream cheese
- 1 cup powdered sugar
- 1 tablespoon heavy whipping cream
- 2 tablespoons maple syrup

Makes 20 - 25

Preparation

1. Preheat the oven to 350°F.

2. Line baking sheets with parchment paper or use silicone baking mats.

3. Prepare cakes: In a bowl, using a rubber spatula, mix flour, baking powder and shredded coconut.

4. Place butter and sugar in a separate mixing bowl. Beat with the mixer's flat beater, until mixture is light and airy. Then add eggs, one at a time, mixing well.

5. Gradually add dry ingredients (prepared in Step 3), sour cream and pineapple cubes. Mix until incorporated.

6. Drop batter onto prepared baking sheets, spacing evenly. Spread batter into approximately 1¼-inch circles.

7. Bake for 7-10 minutes or until cakes are springy to the touch and a toothpick, inserted in the center of a cake, comes out clean.

8. Remove from oven and allow to cool completely on a wire rack.

9. Prepare filling: In a separate bowl, mix cream cheese and powdered sugar with the mixer's flat beater until mixture is light and airy. Add whipping cream and maple syrup (scraping sides of bowl as needed). Mix until the batter is uniform

10. When the cakes are completely cool, spread filling onto the flat side of a cake and top it with another cake. Press gently on top until filling spreads to edges.

Hawaiian Pineapple Coconut Whoopie Pie

Chocolate Oasis

Chocolate Hazelnut (Nutella) Whoopie Pie

In place of Chocolate Hazelnut (Nutella) Cream, you can just use Nutella paste. To enhance the nutty flavor, replace ½ cup flour with ½ cup of roasted hazelnuts.

Ingredients

- 2 cups flour
- 1 teaspoon baking powder
- 1 teaspoon baking soda
- 1 teaspoon lemon juice
- 1½ teaspoon ground cinnamon
- 4 oz butter, at room temperature
- 1¼ cups sugar
- 2 teaspoons vanilla extract or vanilla stick
- 2 eggs
- ½ cup sour cream
- 2 tablespoons heavy whipping cream

Chocolate Hazelnut (Nutella) Cream

- 4 egg whites
- 1 cup sugar
- 3 oz butter at room temperature, cut into cubes
- ½ cup Nutella spread

Chocolate Hazelnut (Nutella) Whoopie Pie

Makes 20 - 25

Preparation

1. Preheat the oven to 350°F.

2. Line baking sheets with parchment paper or use silicone baking mats.

3. **Prepare cakes:** In a bowl, using a rubber spatula, mix flour, baking powder, baking soda and lemon juice.

4. Add ground cinnamon to mixture. Mix until incorporated.

5. Place butter, sugar and vanilla extract (or scraped out vanilla beans) in a separate mixing bowl, beating with the mixer's flat beater until mixture is light and airy. Then add eggs, one at a time, mixing well.

6. Gradually add dry ingredients (prepared in Step 4), sour cream and whipping cream. Mix until incorporated.

7. Drop batter onto prepared baking sheets, spacing evenly. Spread batter into approximately 1¼-inch circles.

8. Bake for 7-10 minutes or until cakes are springy to the touch and a toothpick, inserted in the center of a cake, comes out clean.

9. Remove from oven and allow to cool completely on a wire rack.

10. **Prepare filling:** Pour egg whites and sugar into a bowl placed over a pot of hot water (double boiler). Stir constantly until sugar is dissolved.

11. Transfer to mixing bowl and beat on medium speed, then on high speed, until mixture cools completely and the meringue is set.

12. Gradually add butter and Nutella spread.

13. Mix well until the cream is smooth and uniform.

14. When the cakes are completely cool, spread filling onto the flat side of a cake and top it with another cake. Press gently on top until filling spreads to edges.

Chocolate Mint Whoopie Pie

Makes 20 - 25

You can substitute the mint with basil, vanilla, ginger or any other of your favorite spices.

Another delicious option is to use Cream Cheese and Orange Filling (page 64).

Ingredients

- 1¾ cups flour
- 1½ teaspoons baking powder
- ½ cup cocoa powder
- 4 oz butter, at room temperature
- 1¼ cups sugar
- 1 egg
- 1 cup crème fraiche

French Buttercream Filling

- 4 egg whites
- 1 cup sugar
- 1 teaspoon vanilla extract
- 8 oz butter at room temperature, cut into small cubes

Dark Chocolate Ganâche

- 1 cup whipping cream
- 3 mint leaves
- 10 oz dark chocolate, coarsely chopped

Preparation

1. Preheat the oven to 350°F. Line baking sheets with parchment paper or use silicone baking mats.

2. Prepare cakes: In a bowl, using a rubber spatula, mix flour, baking powder and cocoa powder. Place butter and sugar in a separate mixing bowl. Beat with the mixer's flat beater until mixture is light and airy. Then add the egg and mix well.

3. Gradually add dry ingredients (prepared in Step 2) and crème fraiche. Mix until incorporated. Drop batter onto prepared baking sheets, spacing evenly. Spread batter into approximately 1¼-inch circles.

4. Bake for 7-10 minutes or until cakes are springy to the touch and a toothpick, inserted in the center of a cake, comes out clean. Remove from oven and allow to cool completely on a wire rack.

5. Prepare ganâche: In a small saucepan, heat cream to boiling point, then remove from heat. Place the mint leaves in the cream and let it cool for about 1 hour.

6. Remove mint leaves and heat cream to boiling point again, and then remove from heat. Pour cream over the chopped chocolate. Whisk until the ganâche cream is smooth. Set aside to cool before using.

7. Prepare filling: Pour egg whites and sugar into a bowl placed over a pot of hot water (double boiler). Stir constantly until sugar is dissolved. Beat eggs until mixture cools. Then gradually add vanilla extract and butter. Mix until cream is smooth and uniform.

8. When the cakes are completely cool, spread filling onto the flat side of a cake and top it with another cake. Press gently on top until filling spreads to edges. Place a tablespoon of ganâche on each Whoopie Pie and add fresh mint leaves for decoration.

Chocolate Orange Whoopie Pie

To enjoy the tangy orange flavor with an extra dash of sweetness, use candied orange peels (page 53) instead of orange zest.

Ingredients

- 1¾ cups flour
- 1½ teaspoons baking powder
- ½ cup cocoa powder
- 4 oz butter, at room temperature
- 1¼ cups sugar
- Zest of 1 orange
- 1 egg
- 1 cup crème fraiche

Cream Cheese and Orange Filling

- 8 oz soft cream cheese
- 1 cup powdered sugar
- Zest of 1 orange
- 1 tablespoon orange juice

Makes 20 - 25

Preparation

1. Preheat the oven to 350°F.

2. Line baking sheets with parchment paper or use silicone baking mats.

3. Prepare cakes: In a bowl, using a rubber spatula, mix flour, baking powder and cocoa powder.

4. Place butter, sugar and zest of orange in a separate mixing bowl. Beat with the mixer's flat beater until mixture is light and airy. Then add the egg and mix well.

5. Gradually add dry ingredients (prepared in Step 3) and crème fraiche. Mix until incorporated.

6. Drop batter onto prepared baking sheets, spacing evenly. Spread batter into approximately 1¼-inch circles.

7. Bake for 7-10 minutes or until cakes are springy to the touch and a toothpick, inserted in the center of a cake, comes out clean.

8. Remove from oven and allow to cool completely on a wire rack.

9. Prepare filling: In a separate bowl, mix cream cheese, powdered sugar and orange zest with the mixer's flat beater until mixture is uniform. Add orange juice and mix.

10. When the cakes are completely cool, spread filling onto the flat side of a cake and top it with another cake. Press gently on top until filling spreads to edges.

Double Chocolate Whoopie Pie

You can also use the thick and velvety chocolate ganâche as an additional layer in which to dip half of the Whoopie Pie.

Ingredients

- 1½ cups flour
- 1½ teaspoons baking powder
- ½ cup cocoa powder
- 4 oz butter, at room temperature
- ¾ cup brown sugar
- ½ cup sugar
- 2 eggs
- ½ cup crème fraiche
- ½ cup dark chocolate, finely chopped

Dark Chocolate Ganâche

- 1 cup heavy whipping cream
- 10 oz dark chocolate, coarsely chopped
- 2 oz butter, at room temperature.

Makes 20 - 25

Preparation

1. Preheat the oven to 350°F.

2. Line baking sheets with parchment paper or use silicone baking mats.

3. Prepare cakes: In a bowl, using a rubber spatula, mix flour, baking powder and cocoa powder.

4. Place butter and sugars in a separate mixing bowl. Beat with the mixer's flat beater until mixture is light and airy. Then add eggs, one at a time, mixing well.

5. Gradually add dry ingredients (prepared in Step 3), crème fraiche and dark chopped chocolate. Mix until incorporated.

6. Drop batter onto prepared baking sheets, spacing evenly. Spread batter into approximately 1¼-inch circles.

7. Bake for 7-10 minutes or until cakes are springy to the touch and a toothpick, inserted in the center of a cake, comes out clean.

8. Remove from oven and cool completely on wire rack.

9. Prepare filling: In a small saucepan, bring whipping cream just to a boil. Then remove from heat. Add chopped chocolate and butter.

10. Wait about 1 minute until chocolate melts. Then, using a whisk, mix cream and chocolate in the center of the bowl until ganâche is smooth.

11. Set aside to cool before using. When the cakes are completely cool, spread filling onto the flat side of a cake and top it with another cake. Press gently on top until filling spreads to edges.

Chocolate Coconut Whoopie Pie

Chocolate Coconut Whoopie Pie

Makes 20 - 25

Instead of chopped pistachios, experiment with other tasty options: ground poppy seeds, roasted almonds or shredded coconut. Each of these choices adds a unique and interesting flavor to your Whoopie Pie.

Ingredients

- 1¾ cups flour
- 2 teaspoons baking powder
- ½ cup cocoa powder
- ½ cup chopped pistachios
- 4 oz butter, at room temperature
- 1¼ cups sugar
- 2 eggs
- 1 cup sour cream

White Chocolate Ganâche

- 1 cup heavy whipping cream
- 18 oz white chocolate, coarsely chopped
- 4 oz butter, at room temperature

Preparation

1. Preheat the oven to 350°F.

2. Line baking sheets with parchment paper or use silicone baking mats.

3. Prepare cakes: In a bowl, using a rubber spatula, mix flour, baking powder cocoa powder and chopped pistachios.

4. Place butter and sugar in a separate mixing bowl. Beat with the mixer's flat beater, until mixture is light and airy. Then add eggs, one at a time, mixing well.

5. Gradually add dry ingredients (prepared in Step 3) and sour cream. Mix until incorporated.

6. Drop batter onto prepared baking sheets, spacing evenly. Spread batter into approximately 1¼-inch circles.

7. Bake for 7-10 minutes or until cakes are springy to the touch and a toothpick, inserted in the center of a cake, comes out clean.

8. Remove from oven and allow to cool completely on a wire rack.

9. Prepare filling: In a small saucepan, bring whipping cream just to a boil, and then remove from heat.

10. Add chopped chocolate and butter. Wait about 1 minute until chocolate melts. Then, using a whisk, mix cream and chocolate in the center of the bowl until ganâche is smooth.

11. Set aside to cool before using. When the cakes are completely cool, spread filling onto the flat side of a cake and top it with another cake. Press gently on top until filling spreads to edges.

Chocolate Ganâche Whoopie Pie

Makes 20 - 25

This filling is made of just two ingredients - pure chocolate and heavy whipping cream - ganâche is a chocolate lover's dream.

Keep in mind, if you do not beat the ganâche cream, it will be denser and firmer. It is important to cool it before serving or it will be too runny. It is best to allow it to cool at room temperature, rather than putting it in the refrigerator.

Ingredients

- 1¾ cups flour
- 1½ teaspoons baking powder
- ½ teaspoon salt
- ½ cup cocoa powder
- 4 oz butter
- 1¼ cups sugar
- 1 teaspoon vanilla extract
- 1 egg
- 1 cup sour cream

Dark Chocolate Ganâche

- 1 cup heavy whipping cream
- 10 oz dark chocolate, coarsely chopped

Preparation

1. Preheat the oven to 350°F.

2. Line baking sheets with parchment paper or use silicone baking mats.

3. Prepare cakes: In a bowl, using a rubber spatula, mix flour, baking powder, salt and cocoa powder.

4. Place butter, sugar and vanilla extract in a separate mixing bowl. Beat with the mixer's flat beater, until mixture is smooth and airy. Then add the egg, mixing well.

5. Gradually add dry ingredients (prepared in Step 3) and sour cream. Mix until incorporated. Don't over mix the batter.

6. Drop batter onto prepared baking sheets, spacing evenly. Spread batter into approximately 1¼-inch circles.

7. Bake for 7-10 minutes or until cakes are springy to the touch and a toothpick, inserted in the center of a cake, comes out clean.

8. Remove from oven and allow to cool completely on a wire rack.

9. Prepare filling: In a small saucepan, bring whipping cream just to a boil. Then remove from heat.

10. Add chopped chocolate.

11. Wait about 1 minute until chocolate melts. Then, with a whisk, mix cream and chocolate in the center of the bowl until ganâche is smooth.

12. Set aside to cool before using.

13. When the cakes are completely cool, spread filling onto the flat side of a cake and top it with another cake. Press gently on top until filling spreads to edges.

Marbled Whoopie Pie

For a marble effect, prepare these Whoopie Pies from two batters: vanilla and chocolate. Avoid overmixing the batter and be sure to swirl loosely, so that each Whoopie Pie contains both chocolate and vanilla.

You can also frost with a dark filling or a light frosting. Alternately you could mix the two: half milk chocolate ganâche and half white chocolate ganâche.

Chocolate Base

- 1¾ cups flour
- 1½ teaspoons baking powder
- ½ teaspoon salt
- ½ cup cocoa powder
- 4 oz butter
- 1¼ cups sugar
- 1 teaspoon vanilla extract
- 1 egg
- 1 cup sour cream

Marbled Whoopie Pie

Vanilla Base

- 2¼ cups flour
- 2 teaspoons baking powder
- 4 oz butter
- 1¼ cups sugar
- ½ vanilla stick
- 2 eggs
- ½ cup sour cream

Milk Chocolate Ganâche

- 1 cup heavy whipping cream
- 15 oz milk chocolate, coarsely chopped
- 3 oz butter, at room temperature

Preparation

1. **Prepare Chocolate Whoopie Pie batter** (page 68).

2. **Prepare Vanilla Whoopie Pie batter:** Preheat the oven to 350°F. Line baking sheets with parchment paper or use silicone baking mats.

3. **Prepare cakes:** In a bowl, using a rubber spatula, mix flour, baking powder and cocoa powder.

4. Place butter, sugar and scraped out vanilla beans, in a separate mixing bowl and beat with the mixer's flat beater until mixture is light and airy. Then add eggs, one at a time, mixing well. Gradually add dry ingredients (prepared in Step 3) and sour cream. Mix until incorporated.

5. Divide the batter into two. Using two separate pastry bags, pipe a small amount of each batter onto the baking sheet, so that vanilla batter is on top of chocolate batter, or the other way round. Spread batter into approximately 1¼-inch circles. Use a knife or toothpick to loosely swirl from the center.

6. Bake for 7-10 minutes or until cakes are springy to the touch and a toothpick, inserted in the center of a cake, comes out clean. Remove from oven and allow to cool completely on a wire rack.

7. **Prepare filling:** In a small saucepan, bring whipping cream just to a boil, and then remove from heat. Add chopped chocolate and butter. Wait about 1 minute until chocolate melts. Then, using a whisk, mix cream and chocolate in the center of the bowl until the ganâche is smooth.

8. Set aside to cool before using. When the cakes are completely cool, spread filling onto the flat side of a cake and top it with another cake. Press gently on top until filling spreads to edges.

White & Dark Chocolate Whoopie Pie

White & Dark Chocolate Whoopie Pie

I like to make my own chocolate chips. Use a knife to chop a chocolate block (milk, white or bitter chocolate) into small pieces. Keep chipping until you have the desired size and amount of chips.

For the cream, you can also use milk chocolate or Nutella.

Ingredients

- 1¾ cups flour
- 1½ teaspoons baking powder
- ½ cup cocoa powder
- 4 oz butter, at room temperature
- 1¼ cups sugar
- 1 egg
- 1 cup crème fraiche
- ½ cup white chocolate chips
- ½ cup dark chocolate chips

White Chocolate Ganâche

- 1 cup heavy whipping cream
- 18 oz white chocolate, coarsely chopped
- 4 oz butter, at room temperature

Makes 20 - 25

Preparation

1. Preheat the oven to 350°F.

2. Line baking sheets with parchment paper or use silicone baking mats.

3. Prepare cakes: In a bowl, using a rubber spatula, mix flour, baking powder and cocoa powder.

4. Place butter and sugar in a separate mixing bowl. Beat with the mixer's flat beater, until mixture is smooth and airy. Then add the egg, mixing well.

5. Gradually add dry ingredients (prepared in Step 3), crème fraiche, white chocolate chips and dark chocolate chips. Mix until incorporated.

6. Drop batter onto prepared baking sheets, spacing evenly. Spread batter into approximately 1¼-inch circles.

7. Bake for 7-10 minutes or until cakes are springy to the touch and a toothpick, inserted in the center of a cake, comes out clean.

8. Remove from oven and allow to cool completely on a wire rack.

9. Prepare filling: In a small saucepan, bring whipping cream just to a boil, and then remove from heat.

10. Add chopped chocolate and butter. Wait about 1 minute until chocolate melts. Then, using a whisk, mix cream and chocolate in the center of the bowl until ganâche is smooth.

11. Set aside to cool before using. When the cakes are completely cool, spread filling onto the flat side of a cake and top it with another cake. Press gently on top until filling spreads to edges.

Snickers & Vanilla Cream Whoopie Pie

For variety, prepare the toffee with other favorite roasted nuts, such as walnuts, hazelnuts, or almonds.

For a culinary tickle, try Maple Cream (page 23) or Milk Chocolate Ganâche (page 32).

Ingredients

- 2 cups flour
- 1 teaspoon baking powder
- 1 teaspoon baking soda
- 1 teaspoon lemon juice
- 4 ounces butter, at room temperature
- 1¼ cups sugar
- 2 eggs
- ½ cup sour cream
- 2 tablespoons heavy whipping cream

Butter Toffee Peanut Cream

- ½ cup heavy whipping cream
- ¾ cup sugar
- ½ cup maple syrup
- 2 oz butter, at room temperature
- 1 cup roasted peanuts

Makes 20 - 25

Preparation

1. Preheat the oven to 350°F.

2. Line baking sheets with parchment paper or use silicone baking mats.

3. Prepare cakes: In a bowl, using a rubber spatula, mix flour and baking powder.

4. Add baking soda and lemon juice to mixture. Mix until incorporated.

5. Place butter and sugar in a separate mixing bowl. Beat with the mixer's flat beater, until mixture is light and airy. Then add eggs, one at a time, mixing well.

6. Gradually add dry ingredients mixture (prepared in Step 4), sour cream and whipping cream. Mix until incorporated.

7. Prepare filling: In a saucepan, heat whipping cream just to boil.

8. In a separate saucepan, heat sugar and maple syrup over medium heat, mixing continuously. The filling needs to be thick and caramelized.

9. Carefully pour in whipping cream and butter. Mix well until mixture is smooth. Remove from heat.

10. Stir and add the chopped roasted peanuts, mixing well.

11. Set aside to cool.

12. Drop batter onto prepared baking sheets, spacing evenly. Spread batter into approximately 1¼-inch circles. Using a spoon, place a little toffee on each Whoopie Pie cake.

13. Bake for 7-10 minutes or until cakes are springy to the touch and a toothpick, inserted in the center of a cake, comes out clean.

14. Remove from oven and allow to cool completely on a wire rack.

15. When the cakes are completely cool, spread filling onto the flat side of a cake and top it with another cake. Press gently on top until filling spreads to edges.

Snickers & Vanilla Cream Whoopie Pie

Chocolate Oreo Whoopie Pie

To preserve the cookie's crispness and flavor, add crumbled or crushed cookies to the buttercream. This adds both richness and a crunchy texture.

Makes 20 - 25

Ingredients

- 2 cups flour
- 1½ teaspoons baking powder
- 4 oz butter, at room temperature
- 1¼ cups sugar
- 2 eggs
- ¾ cup sour cream
- 6 Oreo cookies, finely crushed

Dark Chocolate Ganâche

- 1 cup heavy whipping cream
- 10 ounces dark chocolate, coarsely chopped
- 2 oz butter, at room temperature

Preparation

1. Preheat the oven to 350°F.

2. Line baking sheets with parchment paper or use silicone baking mats.

3. Prepare cakes: In a bowl, using a rubber spatula, mix flour and baking powder.

4. Place butter and sugar and in a mixing bowl. Beat with the mixer's flat beater, until mixture is light and airy. Then add the eggs, one at a time, mixing well.

5. Gradually add dry ingredients (prepared in Step 3), sour cream and crushed Oreo cookies. Mix until incorporated.

6. Drop batter onto prepared baking sheets, spacing evenly. Spread batter into approximately 1¼-inch circles.

7. Bake for 7-10 minutes or until cakes are springy to the touch and a toothpick, inserted in the center of a cake, comes out clean.

8. Remove from oven and allow to cool completely on a wire rack.

9. Prepare filling: In a small saucepan, bring whipping cream just to a boil. Then remove from heat. Add chopped chocolate and butter.

10. Wait about 1 minute until chocolate melts. Then, using a whisk, mix cream and chocolate in the center of the bowl until the ganâche is smooth. Set aside to cool before using.

11. When the cakes are completely cool, spread filling onto the flat side of a cake and top it with another cake. Press gently on top until filling spreads to edges.

Chocolate Oreo Whoopie Pie

Chocolate Chip Whoopie Pie

You may use pre-packaged, semi-sweet chocolate chips. Another option is milk chocolate, dark or white chocolate chips, or a mix of all three. You can also try caramel or honey chocolate chips.

Ingredients

- 2 cups flour
- 2 teaspoons baking powder
- ½ cup cocoa powder
- 4 oz butter, at room temperature
- 1¼ cups sugar
- 2 eggs
- 1 cup sour cream
- 1 cup chocolate chips

Dark Chocolate Ganâche

- 1 cup heavy whipping cream
- 10 ounces dark chocolate, coarsely chopped
- 2 oz butter, at room temperature

Makes 20 - 25

Preparation

1. Preheat the oven to 350°F.

2. Line baking sheets with parchment paper or use silicone baking mats.

3. **Prepare cakes:** In a bowl, using a rubber spatula, mix flour, baking powder and cocoa powder.

4. Place butter and sugar in a separate mixing bowl. Beat with the mixer's flat beater, until mixture is light and airy. Then add eggs, one at a time, mixing well.

5. Gradually add dry ingredients (prepared in Step 3), sour cream and chocolate chips. Mix until incorporated.

6. Drop batter onto prepared baking sheets, spacing evenly. Spread batter into approximately 1¼-inch circles.

7. Bake for 7-10 minutes or until cakes are springy to the touch and a toothpick, inserted in the center of a cake, comes out clean. Remove from oven and cool completely on wire rack.

8. **Prepare filling:** In a small saucepan, bring whipping cream just to a boil. Then remove from heat. Add chopped chocolate and butter.

9. Wait about 1 minute until chocolate melts. Then, using a whisk, mix cream and chocolate in the center of the bowl until the ganâche is smooth. Set aside to cool before using.

10. When the cakes are completely cool, spread filling onto the flat side of a cake and top it with another cake. Press gently on top until filling spreads to edges.

Chocolate Peanut Butter Whoopie Pie

You can use salted peanuts or roasted unsalted peanuts for a sweet-salty flavor.

Ingredients

- ¾ cup raw peanuts, finely chopped
- 1½ cups flour
- 1½ teaspoons baking powder
- ½ cup cocoa powder
- 4 oz butter, at room temperature
- 1¼ cups sugar
- 2 eggs
- ½ cup sour cream

Peanut Butter Cream

- 4 oz butter at room temperature
- 1 cup powdered sugar
- ½ cup peanut butter spread

Makes 20 - 25

Preparation

1. Preheat the oven to 350°F. Line baking sheets with parchment paper or use silicone baking mats.

2. Prepare roasted peanuts: Preheat oven to 370°F. Line chilled baking sheet with parchment paper or aluminum foil and fill with raw peanuts. Bake for about 7 minutes, until crust is dry and lightly golden. Transfer to wire rack to cool. When cool, chop the peanuts into small pieces.

3. Prepare cakes: In a bowl, using a rubber spatula, mix flour, baking powder and cocoa powder.

4. Place butter and sugar in a separate mixing bowl. Beat with the mixer's flat beater until mixture is light and airy. Then add eggs, one at a time, mixing well.

5. Gradually add dry ingredients (prepared in Step 3), sour cream and roasted, chopped peanuts. Mix until incorporated.

6. Drop batter onto prepared baking sheets, spacing evenly. Spread batter into approximately 1¼-inch circles.

7. Bake for 7-10 minutes or until cakes are springy to the touch and a toothpick, inserted in the center of a cake, comes out clean. Remove from oven and allow to cool completely on a wire rack.

8. Prepare filling: Cream butter and powdered sugar with the mixer's flat beater, until mixture is light and airy.

9. Add peanut butter spread (scraping sides of bowl as needed), mixing well. When the cakes are completely cool, spread filling onto the flat side of a cake and top it with another cake. Press gently on top until filling spreads to edges.

Chocolate Lavender Whoopie Pie

Chocolate Lavender Whoopie Pie

Herbs and spices each add their own unique and aromatic flair to any dish. Instead of the lavender, try using any of the spices you enjoy, such as sage, anise or mint. When I use mint, I also like to match it up with a green food coloring. Alternately, you can use White Chocolate Ganâche (page 35) to add a fresh new color.

Ingredients

- 1½ cups flour
- 1½ teaspoons baking powder
- ½ cup cocoa powder
- 4 ounces butter, at room temperature
- 1¼ cups sugar
- 2 eggs
- 1½ cups sour cream
- 1 tablespoon dried lavender flowers

French Buttercream Filling

- 4 egg whites
- 1 cup sugar
- 1 teaspoon vanilla extract
- 8 oz butter at room temperature, cut into small cubes
- Purple food coloring

Preparation

1. Preheat the oven to 350°F. Line baking sheets with parchment paper or use silicone baking mats.

2. Prepare cakes: In a bowl, using a rubber spatula, mix flour, baking powder and cocoa powder.

3. Place butter and sugar in a separate mixing bowl. Beat with the mixer's flat beater until mixture is light and airy. Then add eggs, one at a time, mixing well.

4. Gradually add dry ingredients (prepared in Step 3), sour cream and dried lavender. Mix until incorporated.

5. Drop batter onto prepared baking sheets, spacing evenly. Spread batter into approximately 1¼-inch circles.

6. Bake for 7-10 minutes or until cakes are springy to the touch and a toothpick, inserted in the center of a cake, comes out clean. Remove from oven and allow to cool completely on a wire rack.

7. Prepare filling: Pour egg whites and sugar into a bowl placed over a pot of hot water (double boiler). Stir constantly until sugar is dissolved.

8. Beat eggs until mixture cools. Then gradually add vanilla extract and butter. Mix until cream is smooth and uniform.

9. Carefully add purple food coloring and mix until incorporated. (It is best to start with one or two drops, adding as needed.)

10. When the cakes are completely cool, spread filling onto the flat side of a cake and top it with another cake. Press gently on top until filling spreads to edges.

Savory Bites

Beet Whoopie Pie

Use sweet potatoes, carrots, pumpkin or zucchini as a substitute for beets.

Ingredients

- 3 cups flour
- 2 teaspoons baking powder
- 1½ teaspoons salt
- 3 teaspoons sugar
- 8 oz butter, at room temperature
- 2 eggs
- 1 cup sour cream
- 1 beetroot, peeled and thinly grated

Savory Cream Cheese Filling

- 1 cup soft cream cheese
- 2 tablespoons heavy whipping cream

Makes 20 - 25

Preparation

1. Preheat the oven to 350°F.

2. Line baking sheets with parchment paper or use silicone baking mats.

3. Prepare cakes: In a bowl, using a rubber spatula, mix flour, baking powder, salt and sugar.

4. Place butter in a separate mixing bowl, beating with the mixer's flat beater. Then add the eggs, one at a time. Pour in the sour cream and mix well.

5. Gradually add dry ingredients (prepared in Step 3) and grated beetroot. Mix until incorporated into smooth batter.

6. Drop batter onto prepared baking sheets, spacing evenly. Spread batter into approximately 1¼-inch circles.

7. Bake for 10 minutes or until cakes are springy to the touch and a toothpick, inserted in the center of a cake, comes out clean.

8. Remove from oven and cool completely on wire rack.

9. Prepare filling: Beat cream cheese and whipping cream with the mixer's flat beater until mixture is light and airy.

10. When the cakes are completely cool, spread filling onto the flat side of a cake and top it with another cake. Press gently on top until filling spreads to edges.

Beet Whoopie Pie

Cornbread Whoopie Pie

Makes 20 - 25

You can use cooked corn-on-the-cob in place of canned corn. Slide a knife down the cob on all sides to remove the kernels.

To intensify the corn flavor, I like to mix some corn kernels into the batter before baking as well as into the cream before assembling.

Ingredients

- 2½ cups flour
- ½ cup corn flour
- 2 teaspoons baking powder
- 1½ teaspoons salt
- 3 teaspoons sugar
- 8 oz butter, at room temperature
- 2 eggs
- 1 cup sour cream
- 1 cup corn kernels, canned, drained or frozen

Savory Cream Cheese Filling

- 1 cup soft cream cheese
- 2 tablespoons heavy whipping cream

Preparation

1. Preheat the oven to 350°F.

2. Line baking sheets with parchment paper or use silicone baking mats.

3. Prepare cakes: In a bowl, using a rubber spatula, mix flour, corn flour, baking powder, salt and sugar.

4. Place butter in a separate mixing bowl, beating with the mixer's flat beater. Then add the eggs, one at a time. Next pour in sour cream, mixing well.

5. Gradually add dry ingredients (prepared in Step 3) and corn kernels. Mix until incorporated into smooth batter.

6. Drop batter onto prepared baking sheets, spacing evenly. Spread batter into approximately 1¼-inch circles.

7. Bake for 10 minutes or until cakes are springy to the touch and a toothpick, inserted in the center of a cake, comes out clean.

8. Remove from oven and cool completely on wire rack.

9. Prepare filling: Beat cream cheese with whipping cream with the mixer's flat beater until mixture is light and airy.

10. When the cakes are completely cool, spread filling onto the flat side of a cake and top it with another cake. Press gently on top until filling spreads to edges.

Cornbread Whoopie Pie

Smoked Salmon & Chive Whoopie Pie

Smoked Salmon & Chive Whoopie Pie

Makes 20 - 25

You can also add salmon pieces to the cheese filling and serve this luxurious cream alone or as a sandwich salmon spread.

Ingredients

- 3 cups flour
- 2 teaspoons baking powder
- 1 teaspoon salt
- 3 teaspoons sugar
- 8 oz butter, at room temperature
- 2 eggs
- 1 cup crème fraiche
- 1 cup chives, chopped
- 4 oz smoked salmon fillet, cut into cubes

Savory Cream Cheese Filling

- 1 cup cream cheese
- 2 tablespoons heavy whipping cream

Preparation

1. Preheat the oven to 350°F.

2. Line baking sheets with parchment paper or use silicone baking mats.

3. Prepare cakes: In a bowl, using a rubber spatula, mix flour, baking powder, salt and sugar.

4. Place butter in a separate mixing bowl, beating with the mixer's flat beater. Then add the eggs, one at a time. Next pour in the crème fraiche and mix well.

5. Gradually add dry ingredients (prepared in Step 3) and chopped chives. Mix until incorporated.

6. Drop batter onto prepared baking sheets, spacing evenly. Spread batter into approximately 1¼-inch circles.

7. Bake for 10 minutes or until cakes are springy to the touch and a toothpick, inserted in the center of a cake, comes out clean.

8. Remove from oven and cool completely on a wire rack.

9. Prepare filling: Beat cream cheese with whipping cream with the mixer's flat beater until mixture is light and airy.

10. When the cakes are completely cool, spread filling onto the flat side of a cake. Place a piece of salmon and top it with another cake. Press gently on top until filling spreads to edges.

Cheddar Cheese
& Olive Whoopie Pie

In this recipe, you can substitute green olives for black ones.

You can also use any other hard cheese, such as parmesan cheese.

Ingredients

- 3 cups flour
- 2 teaspoons baking powder
- 1 teaspoon salt
- 3 teaspoons sugar
- 8 oz butter, at room temperature
- 2 eggs
- 1 cup sour cream
- ½ cup cheddar cheese, grated
- 1 cup pitted olives, chopped

Savory Cream Cheese Filling

- 1 cup cream cheese
- 2 tablespoons heavy whipping cream

Makes 20 - 25

Preparation

1. Preheat the oven to 350°F.

2. Line baking sheets with parchment paper or use silicone baking mats.

3. Prepare cakes: In a bowl, using a rubber spatula, mix flour, baking powder, salt and sugar.

4. Place butter in a separate mixing bowl, beating with the mixer's flat beater. Then add the eggs, one at a time. Next, pour in the sour cream and mix well.

5. Gradually add dry ingredients (prepared in Step 3), grated cheddar cheese and sliced olives. Mix until incorporated into smooth batter.

6. Drop batter onto prepared baking sheets, spacing evenly. Spread batter into approximately 1¼-inch circles.

7. Bake for 10 minutes or until cakes are springy to the touch and a toothpick, inserted in the center of a cake, comes out clean.

8. Remove from oven and cool completely on a wire rack.

9. Prepare filling: Beat cream cheese with whipping cream with the mixer's flat beater, until mixture is light and airy.

10. When the cakes are completely cool, spread filling onto the flat side of a cake and top it with another cake. Press gently on top until filling spreads to edges.

Anchovy Whoopie Pie

You can add anchovy pieces to the filling. This can be used later as a salty spread accent to a sandwich.

Ingredients

- 3 cups flour
- 2 teaspoons baking powder
- 1 teaspoon salt
- 3 teaspoons sugar
- 8 oz butter, at room temperature
- 2 eggs
- 1 cup crème fraiche
- 4 oz anchovy fillets, drained of oil

Savory Cream Cheese Filling

- 1 cup cream cheese
- 2 tablespoons heavy whipping cream

Preparation

1. Preheat the oven to 350°F.

2. Line baking sheets with parchment paper or use silicone baking mats.

3. **Prepare cakes:** In a bowl, using a rubber spatula, mix flour, baking powder, salt and sugar.

4. Place butter in a separate mixing bowl, beating with the mixer's flat beater. Then add the eggs, one at a time. Next, pour in crème fraiche and mix well.

5. Gradually add dry ingredients (prepared in Step 3). Mix until incorporated.

6. Drop batter onto prepared baking sheets, spacing evenly. Spread batter into approximately 1¼-inch circles.

7. Bake for 10 minutes or until cakes are springy to the touch and a toothpick, inserted in the center of a cake, comes out clean.

8. Remove from oven and cool completely on a wire rack.

9. **Prepare filling:** Beat cream cheese with whipping cream with the mixer's flat beater, until mixture is light and airy.

10. When the cakes are completely cool, spread filling onto the flat side of a cake. Place a piece of anchovy on it and then top it with another cake. Press gently on top until filling spreads to edges.

Mushroom & Goat Cheese Whoopie Pie

Mushroom & Goat Cheese Whoopie Pie

Try using different mushrooms, such as Portobello or champignon. Each kind will add its own distinct flavor and color to your Whoopie Pie. For an especially tender and earthy flavor, use a mixture of forest or exotic mushrooms.

Ingredients

- 2 tablespoons extra-virgin olive oil
- 1 cup champignon mushrooms, thinly sliced
- 3 cups flour
- 2 teaspoons baking powder
- 1 teaspoon salt
- 3 teaspoons sugar
- 8 oz butter, at room temperature
- 2 eggs
- 1 cup sour cream

Goat Cheese Filling

- 1 cup goat cheese
- 3-4 tablespoons heavy whipping cream

Makes 20 - 25

Preparation

1. Preheat the oven to 350°F.

2. Line baking sheets with parchment paper or use silicone baking mats.

3. In a medium frying pan, heat oil over medium heat. Add sliced mushrooms and cook for about 5 minutes, until soft. Remove from heat and allow to cool.

4. Prepare cakes: In a bowl, using a rubber spatula, mix flour, baking powder, salt and sugar.

5. Place butter in a separate mixing bowl, beating with the mixer's flat beater. Then add the eggs, one at a time. Next, pour in the sour cream and mix well.

6. Gradually add dry ingredients (prepared in Step 4) and mushrooms. Mix until incorporated.

7. Drop batter onto prepared baking sheets, spacing evenly. Spread batter into approximately 1¼-inch circles.

8. Bake for 10 minutes or until cakes are springy to the touch and a toothpick, inserted in the center of a cake, comes out clean.

9. Remove from oven and cool completely on a wire rack.

10. Prepare filling: Beat goat cheese with whipping cream with the mixer's flat beater, until mixture is light and airy.

11. When the cakes are completely cool, spread filling onto the flat side of a cake and top it with another cake. Press gently on top until filling spreads to edges.

Kalamata Olive Whoopie Pie

For variety, replace the goat cheese with cream or ricotta cheese.

Ingredients

- 3 cups flour
- 2 teaspoons baking powder
- 1 teaspoon salt
- 3 teaspoons sugar
- 8 oz butter, at room temperature
- 2 eggs
- 1 cup sour cream
- 1 cup pitted Kalamata olives, chopped

Goat Cheese Cream

- 1 cup goat cheese
- 3-4 tablespoons heavy whipping cream

Makes 20 - 25

Preparation

1. Preheat the oven to 350°F.

2. Line baking sheets with parchment paper or use silicone baking mats.

3. Prepare cakes: In a bowl, using a rubber spatula, mix flour, baking powder, salt and sugar.

4. Place butter in a separate mixing bowl, beating with the mixer's flat beater. Then add the eggs, one at a time. Next, pour in the sour cream and mix well.

5. Gradually add dry ingredients (prepared in Step 3) and chopped Kalamata olives. Mix until incorporated into smooth batter.

6. Drop batter onto prepared baking sheets, spacing evenly. Spread batter into approximately 1¼-inch circles.

7. Bake for 10 minutes or until cakes are springy to the touch and a toothpick, inserted in the center of a cake, comes out clean.

8. Remove from oven and cool completely on a wire rack.

9. Prepare filling: Cream goat cheese and whipping cream with the mixer's flat beater, until mixture is light and airy.

10. When the cakes are completely cool, spread filling onto the flat side of a cake and top it with another cake. Press gently on top until filling spreads to edges.

Kalamata Olive Whoopie Pie

Mexican Whoopie Pie

Make this recipe with or without hot peppers. The spicy pepper will add color and intensify the zesty flavors. If you decide to use hot peppers, remove the seeds and the ribs (the white parts inside of the pepper). Wear gloves while handling hot peppers and avoid direct contact.

Ingredients

- 2 tablespoons extra-virgin olive oil
- 1 medium red bell pepper, cut into small cubes
- ½ hot green pepper, cut into small cubes
- 2½ cups flour
- ½ cup corn flour
- 2 teaspoons baking powder
- 1½ teaspoons salt
- 3 teaspoons sugar
- 8 oz butter, at room temperature
- 2 eggs
- 1 cup sour cream

Savory Cream Cheese Filling

- 1 cup cream cheese
- 2 tablespoons heavy whipping cream

Makes 20 - 25

Preparation

1. Preheat the oven to 350°F.

2. Line baking sheets with parchment paper or use silicone baking mats.

3. In a medium frying pan, heat oil over medium heat. Add red and hot green peppers and cook for about 7 minutes, until soft. Remove from heat and allow to cool.

4. Prepare cakes: In a bowl, using a rubber spatula, mix flour, corn flour, baking powder, salt and sugar.

5. Place butter in a separate mixing bowl, beating with the mixer's flat beater. Then add the eggs, one at a time. Next, pour in the sour cream and mix well.

6. Gradually add dry ingredients (prepared in Step 4) and peppers. Mix until incorporated into smooth batter.

7. Drop batter onto prepared baking sheets, spacing evenly. Spread batter into approximately 1¼-inch circles.

8. Bake for 10 minutes or until cakes are springy to the touch and a toothpick, inserted in the center of a cake, comes out clean.

9. Remove from oven and cool completely on a wire rack.

10. Prepare filling: Beat cream cheese with whipping cream with the mixer's flat beater, until mixture is light and airy.

11. When the cakes are completely cool, spread filling onto the flat side of a cake and top it with another cake. Press gently on top until filling spreads to edges.

Spinach & Walnut Whoopie Pie

Makes 20 - 25

In any recipe that calls for nuts, I recommend roasting them first for a few minutes. (page 11)

Ingredients

- 3 tablespoons extra-virgin olive oil
- 2 cups fresh spinach, washed
- 3 cups flour
- 2 teaspoons baking powder
- 1½ teaspoons salt
- 3 teaspoons sugar
- 8 oz butter, at room temperature
- 2 eggs
- 1 cup sour cream
- ½ cup walnuts, crushed

Savory Cream Cheese Filling

- 1 cup cream cheese
- 2 tablespoons heavy whipping cream

Preparation

1. Preheat the oven to 350°F.

2. Line baking sheets with parchment paper or use silicone baking mats.

3. In a medium frying pan, heat oil over medium heat. Add spinach and cook for about 7 minutes, until spinach is soft. Set aside to cool.

4. Prepare cakes: In a bowl, using a rubber spatula, mix flour, baking powder, salt and sugar.

5. Place butter in a separate mixing bowl, beating with the mixer's flat beater. Then add the eggs, one at a time. Next, pour in the sour cream and mix well.

6. Gradually add dry ingredients (prepared in Step 4), cooked spinach and crushed walnuts. Mix until incorporated.

7. Drop batter onto prepared baking sheets, spacing evenly. Spread batter into approximately 1¼-inch circles.

8. Bake for 10 minutes or until cakes are springy to the touch and a toothpick, inserted in the center of a cake, comes out clean.

9. Remove from oven and cool completely on a wire rack.

10. Prepare filling: Beat cream cheese with whipping cream with the mixer's flat beater, until mixture is light and airy.

11. When the cakes are completely cool, spread filling onto the flat side of a cake and top it with another cake. Press gently on top until filling spreads to edges.

Sweet Potato with Thyme Whoopie Pie

Sweet Potato with Thyme Whoopie Pie

The sweet potatoes can be replaced with grated potatoes, beets, carrots or any other root vegetables.

Ingredients

- 3 cups flour
- 2 teaspoons baking powder
- 1½ teaspoons salt
- 3 teaspoons sugar
- 8 oz butter, at room temperature
- 2 eggs
- 1 cup crème fraiche
- 1 sweet potato, thinly grated
- 1 tablespoon fresh thyme leaves

Savory Cream Cheese Filling

- 1 cup cream cheese
- 2 tablespoons heavy whipping cream

Preparation

1. Preheat the oven to 350°F.

2. Line baking sheets with parchment paper or use silicone baking mats.

3. Prepare cakes: In a bowl, using a rubber spatula, mix flour, baking powder, salt and sugar.

4. Place butter in a separate mixing bowl, beating with the mixer's flat beater. Then add the eggs, one at a time. Next, pour in the crème fraiche and mix well.

5. Gradually add dry ingredients (prepared in Step 3), grated sweet potato and thyme leaves. Mix until incorporated into smooth batter.

6. Drop batter onto prepared baking sheets, spacing evenly. Spread batter into approximately 1¼-inch circles.

7. Bake for 10 minutes or until cakes are springy to the touch and a toothpick, inserted in the center of a cake, comes out clean.

8. Remove from oven and cool completely on a wire rack.

9. Prepare filling: Beat cream cheese with whipping cream with the mixer's flat beater, until mixture is light and airy.

10. When the cakes are completely cool, spread filling onto the flat side of a cake and top it with another cake. Press gently on top until filling spreads to edges.

Zucchini with Feta Cheese Whoopie Pie

Zucchini with Feta Cheese Whoopie Pie

Salted hard cheeses, such as Italian parmesan or Spanish manchego, are exquisite substitutes for feta cheese.

Ingredients

- ½ cup raw pine nuts
- 3 cups flour
- 2 teaspoons baking powder
- 1½ teaspoons salt
- 3 teaspoons sugar
- 8 oz butter, at room temperature
- 2 eggs
- 1 cup sour cream
- 1 medium zucchini, finely grated
- 3 oz feta cheese, cut into small cubes

Goat Cheese Cream

- 1 cup goat cheese
- 3-4 tablespoons heavy whipping cream

Makes 20 - 25

Preparation

1. Preheat the oven to 350°F. Line baking sheets with parchment paper or use silicone baking mats.

2. Prepare roasted pine nuts: Preheat oven to 350°F. Line a flat tray with parchment paper or aluminum foil and fill with raw pine nuts. Bake for about 7-10 minutes, until crust is dry and lightly golden. Set aside to cool.

3. Prepare cakes: In a bowl, using a rubber spatula, mix flour, baking powder, salt and sugar.

4. Place butter in a separate mixing bowl, beating with the mixer's flat beater. Then add the eggs, one at a time. Next, pour in the sour cream and mix well.

5. Gradually add dry ingredients (prepared in Step 3), roasted pine nuts, grated zucchini and cubes of feta cheese. Mix until incorporated.

6. Drop batter onto prepared baking sheets, spacing evenly. Spread batter into approximately 1¼-inch circles.

7. Bake for 10 minutes or until cakes are springy to the touch and a toothpick, inserted in the center of a cake, comes out clean.

8. Remove from oven and cool completely on a wire rack.

9. Prepare filling: Beat goat cheese with whipping cream with the mixer's flat beater, until mixture is light and airy.

10. When the cakes are completely cool, spread filling onto the flat side of a cake and top it with another cake. Press gently on top until filling spreads to edges.

Pumpkin Ginger & Cheddar Cheese Whoopie Pie

Makes 20 - 25

If you do not have pumpkin purée, make your own. Place 4 ounces of pumpkin pieces into a pot and cover them with water. Cook until they are tender, drain off the water and mash the cooked pumpkin with a fork.

Ingredients

- 3½ cups flour
- 2½ teaspoons baking powder
- 1½ teaspoons salt
- 3 teaspoons sugar
- 8 oz butter, at room temperature
- 2 eggs
- ¾ cup crème fraiche
- 1 cup pumpkin purée, canned
- 1 tablespoon fresh ginger, thinly grated
- 3 oz cheddar cheese, grated

Savory Cream Cheese Filling

- 1 cup cream cheese
- 2 tablespoons heavy whipping cream

Preparation

1. Preheat the oven to 350°F.

2. Line baking sheets with parchment paper or use silicone baking mats.

3. Prepare cakes: In a bowl, using a rubber spatula, mix flour, baking powder, salt and sugar.

4. Place butter in a separate mixing bowl, beating with the mixer's flat beater. Then add the eggs, one at a time. Next, pour in the crème fraiche and pumpkin puree, mixing well.

5. Gradually add dry ingredients (prepared in Step 3), grated ginger and grated cheddar cheese. Mix until incorporated.

6. Drop batter onto prepared baking sheets, spacing evenly. Spread batter into approximately 1¼-inch circles.

7. Bake for 10 minutes or until cakes are springy to the touch and a toothpick, inserted in the center of a cake, comes out clean.

8. Remove from oven and cool completely on a wire rack.

9. Prepare filling: Beat cream cheese with whipping cream with the mixer's flat beater, until mixture is light and airy.

10. When the cakes are completely cool, spread filling onto the flat side of a cake and top it with another cake. Press gently on top until filling spreads to edges.

Pumpkin Ginger & Cheddar Cheese Whoopie Pie

Sun-Dried Tomato & Basil Whoopie Pie

If fresh basil is not readily available,
you can use dry basil leaves or even pesto.

Ingredients

- 3 cups flour
- 2 teaspoons baking powder
- 1½ teaspoons salt
- 3 teaspoons sugar
- 8 oz butter, at room temperature
- 2 eggs
- 1 cup sour cream
- ½ cup sun-dried tomato paste
- Handful of fresh basil leaves, chopped

Savory Cream Cheese Filling

- 1 cup cream cheese
- 2 tablespoons heavy whipping cream

Makes 20 - 25

Preparation

1. Preheat the oven to 350°F.

2. Line baking sheets with parchment paper or use silicone baking mats.

3. Prepare cakes: In a bowl, using a rubber spatula, mix flour, baking powder, salt and sugar.

4. Place butter in a separate mixing bowl, beating with the mixer's flat beater. Then add the eggs, one at a time. Pour in the sour cream and mix well.

5. Gradually add dry ingredients (prepared in Step 3) sun-dried tomato paste and basil leaves. Mix until incorporated into smooth batter.

6. Drop batter onto prepared baking sheets, spacing evenly. Spread batter into approximately 1¼-inch circles.

7. Bake for 10 minutes or until cakes are springy to the touch and a toothpick, inserted in the center of a cake, comes out clean.

8. Remove from oven and cool completely on wire rack.

9. Prepare filling: Beat cream cheese and whipping cream with the mixer's flat beater, until mixture is light and airy.

10. When the cakes are completely cool, spread filling onto the flat side of a cake and top it with another cake. Press gently on top until filling spreads to edges.

Sun-Dried Tomato & Basil Whoopie Pie

The Classics, Whoopie Style

Classic Marshmallow Whoopie Pie

Classic Marshmallow Whoopie Pie

Butter is the richest flavoring for any dish. However, those who do not like butter, or cannot have it for health reasons, can substitute it with vegetable shortening. Use the same amount of shortening as you would butter.

Ingredients

- 2¼ cups flour
- 2 teaspoons baking powder
- 4 oz butter, at room temperature
- 1¼ cups sugar
- 2 teaspoons vanilla extract or vanilla stick
- 2 eggs
- ½ cup sour cream

Classic Marshmallow Cream

- 8 ounces butter, at room temperature
- 1 cup powdered sugar
- ½ vanilla stick
- 1½ cups marshmallow fluff

Makes 20 - 25

Preparation

1. Preheat the oven to 350°F.

2. Line baking sheets with parchment paper or use silicone baking mats.

3. Prepare cakes: In a bowl, using a rubber spatula, mix flour and baking powder.

4. Place butter, sugar and vanilla extract (or scraped out vanilla beans) in a separate mixing bowl, beating with the mixer's flat beater until mixture is light and airy. Then add eggs, one at a time, mixing well.

5. Gradually add dry ingredients (prepared in Step 3) and sour cream. Mix until incorporated.

6. Drop batter onto prepared baking sheets, spacing evenly. Spread batter into approximately 1¼-inch circles.

7. Bake for 7-10 minutes or until cakes are springy to the touch and a toothpick, inserted in the center of a cake, comes out clean.

8. Remove from oven and allow to cool completely on a wire rack.

9. Prepare filling: Cream butter, powdered sugar and scraped out vanilla beans in an electric mixer with a flat beater for about 5 minutes, until the mixture is light and airy.

10. Add marshmallow fluff and continue beating the mixture, until it has a uniform consistency.

11. When the cakes are completely cool, spread filling onto the flat side of a cake and top it with another cake. Press gently on top until filling spreads to edges.

Classic Chocolate Whoopie Pie

For a special final touch, add an additional layer of chocolate to your Whoopie Pie by making chocolate shavings. Use a cold, firm block of chocolate and a dry grater. Then simply roll the sides of the assembled Whoopie Pie in the chocolate shavings.

For variety, you can also use white or dark chocolate ganâche.

Ingredients

- 1¾ cups flour
- 1½ teaspoons baking powder
- ½ cup cocoa powder
- 4 oz butter, at room temperature
- 1½ cups sugar
- 1 egg
- ¾ cup crème fraiche

Milk Chocolate Ganâche

- 1 cup heavy whipping cream
- 15 ounces milk chocolate, coarsely chopped
- 3 ounces butter, at room temperature

Preparation

1. Preheat the oven to 350°F. Line baking sheets with parchment paper or use silicone baking mats.

2. Prepare cakes: In a bowl, using a rubber spatula, mix flour, baking powder and cocoa powder.

3. Place butter and sugar in a separate mixing bowl, beating with the mixer's flat beater until mixture is light and airy. Then add the egg, mixing well.

4. Gradually add dry ingredients (prepared in Step 3) and crème fraiche. Mix until incorporated.

5. Drop batter onto prepared baking sheets, spacing evenly. Spread batter into approximately 1¼-inch circles.

6. Bake for 7-10 minutes or until cakes are springy to the touch and a toothpick, inserted in the center of a cake, comes out clean.

7. Remove from oven and allow to cool completely over a wire rack.

8. Prepare filling: In a small saucepan, bring whipping cream just to a boil. Then remove from heat.

9. Add chopped chocolate and butter.

10. Wait about 1 minute until chocolate melts. Then, using a whisk, mix cream and chocolate in the center of the bowl until the ganâche is smooth.

11. Set aside to cool before using. When the cakes are completely cool, spread filling onto the flat side of a cake and top it with another cake. Press gently on top until filling spreads to edges.

Black Forest Whoopie Pie

I like to roll the assembled Whoopie Pies in chocolate shavings.

Makes 20 - 25

Ingredients

- 1¾ cups flour
- 1½ teaspoons baking powder
- ½ cup cocoa powder
- 4 oz butter, at room temperature
- 1¼ cups sugar
- 1 egg
- ¾ cup crème fraiche
- ½ cup cherry jam

French Buttercream Filling

- 4 egg whites
- 1 cup sugar
- 1 teaspoon vanilla extract
- 8 ounces butter at room temperature, cut into small cubes

Decoration

- 2 oz dark chocolate, finely grated

Preparation

1. Preheat the oven to 350°F. Line baking sheets with parchment paper or use silicone baking mats.

2. Prepare cakes: In a bowl, using a rubber spatula, mix flour, baking powder and cocoa powder.

3. Place butter and sugar in a separate mixing bowl, beating with the mixer's flat beater until mixture is light and airy. Then add the egg, mixing well.

4. Gradually add dry ingredients (prepared in Step 2) and crème fraiche. Mix until incorporated.

5. Drop batter onto prepared baking sheets, spacing evenly. Spread batter into approximately 1¼-inch circles.

6. Bake for 7-10 minutes or until cakes are springy to the touch and a toothpick, inserted in the center of a cake, comes out clean. Remove from oven and allow to cool completely on a wire rack.

7. Prepare filling: Pour egg whites and sugar into a bowl placed over a pot of hot water (double boiler). Stir constantly until sugar is dissolved.

8. Beat eggs until mixture cools. Then gradually add vanilla extract and butter. Mix until cream is smooth and uniform.

9. When the cakes are completely cool, roll in chocolate shavings and spread cherry jam on each Whoopie Pie. Add the remaining jam to the French buttercream, spread this filling onto the flat side of a cake and top it with another cake.

10. Press gently on top until filling spreads to edges.

Red Velvet Whoopie Pie

To add an additional red textured coating, take one or two already-baked Red Velvet Whoopie cakes and crumble them into small pieces. Next, simply press and roll the edges of the assembled Whoopie Pie in the crumbs.

Ingredients

- 1 cup flour
- ½ teaspoon baking powder
- 2 tablespoons cocoa powder
- ½ teaspoon white vinegar or orange vinegar
- ½ teaspoon baking soda
- ½ cup crème fraiche
- 4 oz butter, at room temperature
- ¾ cup sugar
- 1 egg
- 1 tablespoon red food coloring

French Buttercream Filling

- 4 egg whites
- 1 cup sugar
- 1 teaspoon vanilla extract
- 8 oz butter at room temperature, cut into small cubes

Makes 20 - 25

Preparation

1. Preheat the oven to 350°F. Line baking sheets with parchment paper or use silicone baking mats.

2. Prepare cakes: In a bowl, using a rubber spatula, mix flour, baking powder and cocoa powder.

3. In a separate bowl, mix vinegar and baking soda. Add the crème fraiche, mixing well.

4. Place butter and sugar in a separate mixing bowl, beating with the mixer's flat beater until mixture is light, airy and creamy. Then add the egg and mix well.

5. Gradually add dry ingredients (prepared in Step 2) and crème fraiche mixture. Next, carefully add red food coloring and mix until incorporated. (It is best to start with one or two drops, adding as needed.)

6. Drop batter onto prepared baking sheets, spacing evenly. Spread batter into approximately 1¼-inch circles.

7. Bake for 7-10 minutes or until cakes are springy to the touch and a toothpick, inserted in the center of a cake, comes out clean. Remove from oven and allow to cool completely on a wire rack.

8. Prepare filling: Pour egg whites and sugar into a bowl placed over a pot of hot water (double boiler). Stir constantly until sugar is dissolved.

9. Beat eggs until mixture cools. Then gradually add vanilla extract and butter. Mix until cream is smooth and uniform.

10. When the cakes are completely cool, spread filling onto the flat side of a cake and top it with another cake. Press gently on top until filling spreads to edges.

Red Velvet Whoopie Pie

Tiramisu
Whoopie Pie

In this recipe an instant coffee powder can be used instead of the coffee extract. Simply dissolve 1 tablespoon of instant coffee powder in hot water. Be sure not to add the hot liquid directly to the batter. Allow it to cool first.

Another option is to use Kahlua or any other coffee liqueur.

Ingredients

- 2 cups flour
- 1½ teaspoons baking powder
- 4 oz butter, at room temperature
- 1¼ cups sugar
- 2 eggs
- ½ cup sour cream
- 2 tablespoons coffee extract

Tiramisu, Mascarpone Cheese & Coffee Cream

- 2 oz butter, at room temperature
- 4 oz mascarpone cheese
- 1½ cups powdered sugar
- 1 tablespoon coffee extract (or 1 teaspoon instant coffee, dissolved in water)

Preparation

1. Preheat the oven to 350°F.

2. Line baking sheets with parchment paper or use silicone baking mats.

3. Prepare cakes: In a bowl, using a rubber spatula, mix flour and baking powder.

4. Place butter and sugar in a separate mixing bowl, beating with the mixer's flat beater until mixture is light and airy. Then add eggs, one at a time, mixing well.

5. Gradually add dry ingredients (prepared in Step 3), sour cream and coffee extract. Mix until incorporated.

6. Drop batter onto prepared baking sheets, spacing evenly. Spread batter into approximately 1¼-inch circles.

7. Bake for 7-10 minutes or until cakes are springy to the touch and a toothpick, inserted in the center of a cake, comes out clean.

8. Remove from oven and allow to cool completely on a wire rack.

9. Prepare filling: Beat butter, mascarpone cheese, powdered sugar and coffee extract with the mixer's flat beater, until mixture is uniform.

10. When the cakes are completely cool, spread filling onto the flat side of a cake and top it with another cake. Press gently on top until filling spreads to edges.

Lemon Yogurt with Strawberry Jam Whoopie Pie

Makes 20 - 25

For variety, in place of yogurt, use sour cream or crème fraiche.

Ingredients

- 2 cups flour
- 1½ teaspoons baking powder
- 4 oz butter, at room temperature
- 1¼ cups sugar
- Zest of 1 lemon
- 2 eggs
- ⅓ cup unflavored yogurt

French Buttercream Filling

- 4 egg whites
- 1 cup sugar
- 1 teaspoon vanilla extract
- 8 oz butter at room temperature, cut into small cubes
- ⅓ cup strawberry jam

Preparation

1. Preheat the oven to 350°F.

2. Line baking sheets with parchment paper or use silicone baking mats.

3. Prepare cakes: In a bowl, using a rubber spatula, mix flour and baking powder.

4. Place butter, sugar and zest of lemon in a separate mixing bowl, beating with the mixer's flat beater until mixture is light, airy and creamy. Then add eggs, one at a time, mixing well.

5. Gradually add dry ingredients (prepared in Step 3) and yogurt. Mix until incorporated.

6. Drop batter onto prepared baking sheets, spacing evenly. Spread batter into approximately 1¼-inch circles.

7. Bake for 7-10 minutes or until cakes are springy to the touch and a toothpick, inserted in the center of a cake, comes out clean.

8. Remove from oven and allow to cool completely on a wire rack.

9. Prepare filling: Pour egg whites and sugar into a bowl placed over a pot of hot water (double boiler). Stir constantly until sugar is dissolved.

10. Beat eggs until mixture cools. Then gradually add vanilla extract and butter. Mix until cream is smooth and uniform. Add strawberry jam into the cream, mixing well.

11. When the cakes are completely cool, spread filling onto the flat side of a cake and top it with another cake. Press gently on top until filling spreads to edges.

Rainbow Whoopie Pie

To simplify the process, do not pipe or spread each cookie with all four colors at once. First, pipe or spread the whole Whoopie Pies tray with one color, then continue with the second color and so on.

Ingredients

- 2 cups flour
- 1½ teaspoons baking powder
- 4 oz butter, at room temperature
- 1¼ cups sugar
- 2 teaspoons vanilla extract or vanilla stick
- 2 eggs
- ½ cup sour cream
- Food coloring (yellow, red, pink and purple)

French Buttercream Filling

- 4 egg whites
- 1 cup sugar
- 1 teaspoon vanilla extract
- 8 oz butter at room temperature, cut into small cubes

Preparation

1. Preheat the oven to 350°F.

2. Line baking sheets with parchment paper or use silicone baking mats.

3. Prepare cakes: In a bowl, using a rubber spatula, mix flour and baking powder.

4. Place butter and sugar and vanilla extract (or scraped out vanilla beans) in a separate mixing bowl. Beat with the mixer's flat beater until mixture is light and airy. Then add the eggs, one at a time, mixing well.

5. Gradually add dry ingredients (prepared in Step 3) and sour cream. Mix until incorporated.

6. Divide batter into four parts in separate bowls. Add a different food coloring to each bowl. It is always best to start with one or two drops, checking the color and adding more if necessary.

7. Transfer batter into four pastry bags. Pipe a small amount of each batter next to each other on the baking sheet in approximately 1¼-inch circles. Then, with a knife or toothpick, loosely swirl from the center to combine all four colors.

8. Bake for 7-10 minutes or until cakes are springy to the touch and a toothpick, inserted in the center of a cake, comes out clean.

9. Remove from oven and allow to cool completely on a wire rack.

10. Prepare filling: Pour egg whites and sugar into a bowl placed over a pot of hot water (double boiler). Stir constantly until sugar is dissolved.

Rainbow Whoopie Pie

11. Beat eggs until mixture cools.
Then gradually add vanilla extract and butter.
Mix until cream is smooth and uniform.

12. When the cakes are completely cool,
spread filling onto the flat side of a cake and top it
with another cake. Press gently on top until filling
spreads to edges.

Dulce De Leche Whoopie Pie

Using this recipe, you can actually make Alfajores cookies. Simply press and roll the edges of each Whoopie Pie into shredded coconut. In place of Dulce de Leche Cream, you can use readymade Dulce de Leche, straight from the jar.

Ingredients

- 2 cups flour
- 1 teaspoons baking powder
- 4 oz butter, at room temperature
- ¾ cup sugar
- ½ cup brown sugar
- 2 teaspoons vanilla extract or vanilla stick
- 2 eggs
- ½ cup sour cream

Dulce de Leche Cream

- 1 cup milk
- 1 teaspoon vanilla extract
- ½ cup sugar
- 4 egg yolks
- 2 tablespoons cornstarch
- 1 tablespoon flour
- ½ cup Dulce de Leche paste

Decoration

- ½ cup shredded coconut

Dulce De Leche Whoopie Pie

Preparation

1. Preheat the oven to 350°F.

2. Line baking sheets with parchment paper or use silicone baking mats.

3. Prepare cakes: In a bowl, using a rubber spatula, mix flour and baking powder.

4. Place butter, sugar and vanilla extract (or scraped out vanilla beans) in a separate mixing bowl, beating with the mixer's flat beater until mixture is light and airy. Then add eggs, one at a time, mixing well.

5. Gradually add dry ingredients (prepared in Step 3) and sour cream. Mix until incorporated. Avoid overmixing the batter.

6. Drop batter onto prepared baking sheets, spacing evenly. Spread batter into approximately 1¼-inch circles.

7. Bake for 7-10 minutes or until cakes are springy to the touch and a toothpick, inserted in the center of a cake, comes out clean.

8. Remove from oven and allow to cool completely on a wire rack.

9. Prepare filling: In a saucepan, heat milk and vanilla extract just to boiling, and then remove from heat.

10. In a bowl, whisk sugar and egg yolks. Gradually add cornstarch and flour, mixing well until mixture is uniform. Pour ⅓ of the milk mixture into the bowl, while stirring constantly.

11. Heat remaining milk mixture over a low heat, add egg mixture and stir constantly. Cook until cream firms and thickens.

12. Remove from heat and stir. Add Dulce de Leche paste and mix.

13. Press a piece of plastic wrap against surface to create an airtight seal and refrigerate.

14. When the cakes are completely cool, spread filling onto the flat side of a cake and top it with another cake. Press gently on top until filling spreads to edges.

Peanut Butter & Strawberry Jam Whoopie Pie

Roasted salted peanuts, cashews, almonds, or any of your favorite nuts will suit this recipe and satisfy your personal craving.

Ingredients

- ¾ cup raw peanuts, chopped
- 2 cups flour
- 1½ teaspoons baking powder
- 4 oz butter, at room temperature
- 1¼ cups sugar
- 2 eggs
- ½ cup sour cream
- ⅓ cup strawberry jam

Peanut Butter Filling

- 4 ounces butter, at room temperature
- ¾ cup powdered sugar
- ½ cup peanut butter spread

Makes 20 - 25

Preparation

1. Preheat the oven to 350°F.

2. Line baking sheets with parchment paper or use silicone baking mats.

3. **Prepare roasted peanuts:** Preheat oven to 370°F. Line chilled baking sheet with parchment paper or aluminum foil and fill with raw peanuts. Bake for about 7 minutes, until crust is dry and lightly golden. Transfer to wire rack to cool. When cool, chop the peanuts into small pieces.

4. **Prepare cakes:** In a bowl, using a rubber spatula, mix flour and baking powder.

5. Place butter and sugar in a separate mixing bowl, beating with the mixer's flat beater until mixture is light and airy. Then add eggs, one at a time, mixing well.

6. Gradually add dry ingredients (prepared in Step 4), sour cream and roasted peanuts. Mix until incorporated.

7. Drop batter onto prepared baking sheets, spacing evenly. Spread batter into approximately 1¼-inch circles.

8. Bake for 7-10 minutes or until cakes are springy to the touch and a toothpick, inserted in the center of a cake, comes out clean.

9. Remove from oven and allow to cool completely on a wire rack.

10. **Prepare filling:** Cream butter with powdered sugar with the mixer's flat beater, until mixture is light and airy.

Peanut Butter & Strawberry Jam Whoopie Pie

11. Add peanut butter spread and mix well, using a rubber spatula (scraping sides of bowl as needed).

12. When the cakes are completely cool, spread filling onto the flat side of a cake. Place ½ teaspoon of strawberry jam and top it with another cake. Press gently on top until filling spreads to edges.

Carrot & Cream Cheese Whoopie Pie

Carrot & Cream Cheese Whoopie Pie

Keep in mind that nutmeg is highly aromatic and dominant, so use it in moderation.

Ingredients

- 1¾ cups flour
- 2 teaspoons baking powder
- ½ cup shredded coconut
- 1 teaspoon ground cinnamon
- ½ teaspoon ground ginger or fresh ginger, thinly grated
- Pinch of nutmeg
- Pinch of ground cloves
- 4 oz butter, at room temperature
- 1¼ cups brown sugar
- 2 eggs
- ½ cup sour cream
- 1 carrot, thinly grated
- ½ cup pecans, finely chopped

Cream Cheese Filling

- 8 oz cream cheese
- 1 cup powdered sugar
- 1 tablespoon heavy whipping cream
- 1 teaspoon lemon or orange juice

Preparation

1. Preheat the oven to 350°F. Line baking sheets with parchment paper or use silicone baking mats.

2. **Prepare cakes:** In a bowl, using a rubber spatula, mix flour and baking powder.

3. Using a rubber spatula, mix dry ingredients, shredded coconut, ground cinnamon, ginger, nutmeg and ground cloves.

4. Place butter and sugar in a separate mixing bowl, beating with the mixer's flat beater until mixture is light and airy. Then add eggs, one at a time, mixing well.

5. Gradually add dry ingredients (prepared in Step 3), sour cream, grated carrot and chopped pecans. Mix until incorporated.

6. Drop batter onto prepared baking sheets, spacing evenly. Spread batter into approximately 1¼-inch circles.

7. Bake for 7-10 minutes or until cakes are springy to the touch and a toothpick, inserted in the center of a cake, comes out clean.

8. Remove from oven and allow to cool completely on a wire rack.

9. **Prepare filling:** Mix cream cheese and powdered sugar in an electric mixer with a flat beater, until mixture is light and airy.

10. Add whipping cream and lemon or orange juice, scraping sides of bowl as needed. Continue beating until mixture is smooth and uniform.

11. When the cakes are completely cool, spread filling onto the flat side of a cake and top it with another cake. Press gently on top until filling spreads to edges.

Mocha Whoopie Pie

You can use concentrated espresso, instant coffee or any other coffee liqueur in this recipe. Coffee extracts can be used too, but then the coffee flavor will be more dominant. Be sure NOT to add the hot espresso liquid directly to the batter. Allow it to cool first. For future reference, make note of the amount of coffee you used to achieve the taste you prefer.

Ingredients

- 1½ cups flour
- 1½ teaspoons baking powder
- ½ cup cocoa powder
- 2 tablespoons instant coffee powder + 1 tablespoon boiling water
- 4 oz butter, at room temperature
- ¾ cup sugar
- ½ cup brown sugar
- 1 egg
- ½ cup crème fraiche

Mocha Cream

- 4 egg whites
- 1 cup sugar
- 1 teaspoon vanilla extract
- 8 oz butter at room temperature, cut into cubes
- 2 tablespoons instant coffee powder + 1 tablespoon boiling water
- 4 oz dark chocolate, coarsely chopped

Mocha Whoopie Pie

Makes 20 - 25

Preparation

1. Preheat the oven to 350°F.

2. Line baking sheets with parchment paper or use silicone baking mats.

2. Prepare cakes: In a bowl, using a rubber spatula, mix flour, baking powder and cocoa powder

4. Dissolve instant coffee powder in boiling water and mix. Set aside to cool.

5. Place butter and sugars in a separate mixing bowl, beating with the mixer's flat beater until mixture is light, airy and creamy. Then add the egg, mixing well.

6. Gradually add dry ingredients (prepared in Step 3), crème fraiche and instant coffee mixture (prepared in Step 4). Mix until incorporated.

7. Drop batter onto prepared baking sheets, spacing evenly. Spread batter into approximately 1¼-inch circles.

8. Bake for 7-10 minutes or until cakes are springy to the touch and a toothpick, inserted in the center of a cake, comes out clean.

9. Remove from oven and allow to cool completely on a wire rack.

10. Prepare filling: Pour egg whites and sugar into a bowl and place over a pot of hot water (double boiler). Stir constantly until sugar is dissolved.

11. Beat the egg whites until mixture cools. Gradually add vanilla extract and butter.

12. Dissolve instant coffee powder in boiling water.

13. Pour chocolate into a bowl and place over a pot of hot water (double boiler), stirring constantly until chocolate is melted. Avoid all contact with water—even a few droplets. (Otherwise the chocolate will separate and become unusable.) Add this mixture to the pot and stir well until cream is smooth.

14. Add this mixture and instant coffee mixture (prepared in Step 12) to the cream and stir well, until cream is smooth.

15. When the cakes are completely cool, spread filling onto the flat side of a cake and top it with another cake. Press gently on top until filling spreads to edges.

Holidays & Special Occasions

Halloween Pumpkin Whoopie Pie

Bring in the holiday spirit and your own creativity by replacing the gooseberries with any of your favorite berries, or by using apple purée instead of pumpkin purée.

Ingredients

- 2½ cups flour
- 1 teaspoon baking soda
- 4 oz butter, at room temperature
- 1¼ cups sugar
- 2 eggs
- ½ cup pumpkin puree

Cream Cheese Filling

- 8 ounces cream cheese
- 1 cup powdered sugar
- 1 tablespoon heavy whipping cream
- 1 teaspoon lemon or orange juice

Makes 20 - 25

Preparation

1. Preheat the oven to 350°F.

2. Line baking sheets with parchment paper or use silicone baking mats.

3. **Prepare cakes:** In a bowl, using a rubber spatula, mix flour and baking powder.

4. Place butter and sugar in a separate mixing bowl. Beat with the mixer's flat beater, until mixture is light and airy. Then add eggs, one at a time, mixing well.

5. Gradually add dry ingredients (prepared in Step 3) and pumpkin puree. Mix until incorporated.

6. Drop batter onto prepared baking sheets, spacing evenly. Spread batter into approximately 1¼-inch circles.

7. Bake for 7-10 minutes or until cakes are springy to the touch and a toothpick, inserted in the center of a cake, comes out clean.

8. Remove from oven and allow to cool completely on a wire rack.

9. **Prepare filling:** Mix cream cheese and powdered sugar in an electric mixer with a flat beater, until mixture is light and airy.

10. Add whipping cream and lemon or orange juice, scraping sides of bowl as needed. Continue beating until consistency is smooth and uniform.

11. When the cakes are completely cool, spread filling onto the flat side of a cake and top it with another cake. Press gently on top until filling spreads to edges.

Christmas Gingerbread Whoopie Pie

In this special holiday recipe, you can also use sour cream or butter cream.

Ingredients

- 2¼ cups flour
- 2 teaspoons baking powder
- 1 teaspoon ground cinnamon
- ¼ teaspoon ground cloves
- ½ ground ginger
- 4 oz butter, at room temperature
- 1¼ cups sugar
- 2 eggs
- ¼ cup crème fraiche
- ¼ cup candied ginger

Maple Cream

- 8 ounces soft cream cheese
- 1 cup powdered sugar
- 1 tablespoon heavy whipping cream
- 2 tablespoons maple syrup

Makes 20 - 25

Preparation

1. Preheat the oven to 350°F. Line baking sheets with parchment paper or use silicone baking mats.

2. **Prepare cakes:** In a bowl, using a rubber spatula, mix flour and baking powder.

3. Add ground cinnamon, ground cloves, and ground ginger, mixing well.

4. Place butter and sugar in a separate mixing bowl. Beat with the mixer's flat beater, until mixture is light and airy. Then add eggs, one at a time, mixing well.

5. Gradually add dry ingredients (prepared in Step 3), crème fraiche and candied ginger. Mix until incorporated.

6. Drop batter onto prepared baking sheets, spacing evenly. Spread batter into approximately 1¼-inch circles.

7. Bake for 7-10 minutes or until cakes are springy to the touch and a toothpick, inserted in the center of a cake, comes out clean.

8. Remove from oven and allow to cool completely on a wire rack.

9. **Prepare filling:** In a separate bowl, mix cream cheese and powdered sugar with the mixer's flat beater, until mixture is light and airy. Add whipping cream and maple syrup (scraping sides of bowl as needed). Mix well until the batter is uniform.

10. When the cakes are completely cool, spread filling onto the flat side of a cake and top it with another cake. Press gently on top until filling spreads to edges.

Christmas Gingerbread Whoopie Pie

St. Patrick's Day Whoopie Pie

When using a vanilla stick, ensure that all the vanilla beans are carefully scraped out. Cut the vanilla stick in half lengthwise, then split vanilla stick and scrape the beans out, using the edge of a knife.

Ingredients

- 2¼ cups flour
- 2 teaspoons baking powder
- 4 oz butter, at room temperature
- 1¼ cups sugar
- 2 teaspoons vanilla extract or ½ vanilla stick
- 2 eggs
- ½ cup crème fraiche
- 1 tablespoon green food coloring

Classic Marshmallow Cream

- 8 oz butter, at room temperature
- 1 cup powdered sugar
- ½ vanilla stick
- 1½ cups marshmallow fluff

Makes 20 - 25

Preparation

1. Preheat the oven to 350°F. Line baking sheets with parchment paper or use silicone baking mats.

2. Prepare cakes: In a bowl, using a rubber spatula, mix flour and baking powder.

3. Place butter, sugar and vanilla extract (or scraped vanilla beans) in a separate mixing bowl. Beat with the mixer's flat beater, until mixture is light and airy. Then add eggs, one at a time, mixing well.

4. Gradually add dry ingredients (prepared in Step 2) and crème fraiche. Carefully add green food coloring and mix until incorporated. (It is best to start with one or two drops, adding as needed.)

5. Drop batter onto prepared baking sheets, spacing evenly. Spread batter into approximately 1¼-inch circles.

6. Bake for 7-10 minutes or until cakes are springy to the touch and a toothpick, inserted in the center of a cake, comes out clean.

7. Remove from oven and allow to cool completely on a wire rack.

8. Prepare filling: Beat butter, powdered sugar and scraped out vanilla beans with the mixer's flat beater for about 5 minutes, until mixture is light and airy.

9. Add marshmallow fluff and continue beating mixture until consistency is uniform.

10. When the cakes are completely cool, spread filling onto the flat side of a cake and top it with another cake. Press gently on top until filling spreads to edges.

St. Patrick's Day Whoopie Pie

Easter Whoopie Pie

To make an Easter nest, divide sugar dough into three pieces. Color each piece in a different food coloring and prepare a small ball out of each one. Put three small cookie balls on the top of each Whoopie Pie.

You can also use Milk Chocolate Ganâche (page 32). Simply dip the top of the cookies in ganâche. Allow them to cool and the chocolate to set.

Ingredients

- 2 cups flour
- 2 teaspoons baking powder
- 4 oz butter, at room temperature
- 1¼ cups sugar
- 2 eggs
- ½ cup crème fraiche

Cream Cheese Filling

- 8 ounces cream cheese
- 1 cup powdered sugar
- 1 tablespoon heavy whipping cream
- 1 teaspoon lemon or orange juice

Decoration

- 3 ounces sugar dough
- Food coloring (pink, purple and yellow)

Preparation

1. Preheat the oven to 350°F.

2. Line baking sheets with parchment paper or use silicone baking mats.

3. Prepare cakes: In a bowl, using a rubber spatula, mix flour and baking powder.

4. Place butter and sugar in a separate mixing bowl, beating with the mixer's flat beater until mixture is light and airy. Then add eggs, one at a time, mixing well.

5. Gradually add dry ingredients (prepared in Step 3) and crème fraiche. Mix until incorporated.

6. Drop batter onto prepared baking sheets, spacing evenly. Spread batter into approximately 1¼-inch circles.

7. Bake for 7-10 minutes or until cakes are springy to the touch and a toothpick, inserted in the center of a cake, comes out clean.

8. Remove from oven and allow to cool completely.

9. Prepare filling: Beat cream cheese and powdered sugar in an electric mixer with a flat beater, until mixture is light and airy.

10. Add whipping cream and lemon or orange juice, scraping sides of bowl as needed. Continue beating until consistency is uniform.

11. When the cakes are completely cool, spread filling onto the flat side of a cake and top it with another cake. Press gently on top until filling spreads to edges.

Gluten-Free Passover Whoopie Pie

Use shredded coconut, poppy seeds or any other finely ground nut instead of flour. This recipe is especially suited for anyone seeking kosher or dairy-free dessert alternatives.

For variety, you can use Maple Cream (page 23) or Cream Cheese Filling (page 33).

Ingredients

- 1½ cups gluten-free flour
- 2 teaspoons baking powder
- 4 oz butter, at room temperature
- ¾ cup sugar
- ½ cup brown sugar
- 2 teaspoons vanilla extract or vanilla stick
- 2 eggs
- ½ cup crème fraiche
- ½ cup ground blanched almonds
- ½ cup white chocolate chips

French Buttercream Filling

- 4 egg whites
- 1 cup sugar
- 1 teaspoon vanilla extract
- 8 oz butter at room temperature, cut into small cubes

Makes 20 - 25

Preparation

1. Preheat the oven to 350°F. Line baking sheets with parchment paper or use silicone baking mats.

2. Prepare cakes: In a bowl, using a rubber spatula, mix gluten-free flour and baking powder.

3. Place butter, sugars and vanilla extract (or scraped out vanilla beans) in a separate mixing bowl, beating with the mixer's flat beater until mixture is light and airy. Then add eggs, one at a time, mixing well.

4. Gradually add dry ingredients (prepared in Step 2), crème fraiche, ground almonds and chocolate chips. Mix until incorporated.

5. Drop batter onto prepared baking sheets, spacing evenly. Spread batter into approximately 1¼-inch circles.

6. Bake for 7-10 minutes or until cakes are springy to the touch and a toothpick, inserted in the center of a cake, comes out clean.

7. Remove from oven and allow to cool completely on a wire rack.

8. Prepare filling: Pour egg whites and sugar into a bowl placed over a pot of hot water (double boiler). Stir constantly until sugar is dissolved.

9. Beat eggs until mixture cools. Then gradually add vanilla extract and butter. Mix until cream is smooth and uniform.

10. When the cakes are completely cool, spread filling onto the flat side of a cake and top it with another cake. Press gently on top until filling spreads to edges.

4th of July Whoopie Pie

For the perfect flag, roll and press the assembled Whoopie Pie in red or white star sprinkles.

For variety, use Maple Cream (page 23) or Classic Marshmallow Cream (page 23).

Ingredients

- 2 cups flour
- 1½ teaspoons baking powder
- 4 oz butter, at room temperature
- ¾ cup sugar
- ½ cup brown sugar
- Zest of 1 lemon
- 2 eggs
- ½ cup crème fraiche
- Blue food coloring

Cream Cheese Filling

- 8 ounces cream cheese
- 1 cup powdered sugar
- 1 tablespoon heavy whipping cream
- 1 teaspoon lemon or orange juice

Decoration

- ½ cup red or white star sprinkles

Makes 20 - 25

Preparation

1. Preheat the oven to 350°F. Line baking sheets with parchment paper or use silicone baking mats.

2. **Prepare cakes:** In a bowl, using a rubber spatula, mix flour and baking powder.

3. Place butter, sugars and zest of lemon in a separate mixing bowl, beating with the mixer's flat beater until mixture is light and airy. Then add eggs, one at a time, mixing well.

4. Gradually add dry ingredients (prepared in Step 2) and crème fraiche.

5. Carefully add blue food coloring and mix until incorporated. (It is best to start with one or two drops, adding as needed.)

6. Drop batter onto prepared baking sheets, spacing evenly. Spread batter into approximately 1¼-inch circles.

7. Bake for 7-10 minutes or until cakes are springy to the touch and a toothpick, inserted in the center of a cake, comes out clean. Remove from oven and allow to cool completely on a wire rack.

8. **Prepare filling:** Beat cream cheese and powdered sugar in an electric mixer with the mixer's flat beater, until mixture is light and airy.

9. Add whipping cream and lemon or orange juice, scraping sides of bowl as needed. Continue beating until consistency is uniform.

10. When the cakes are completely cool, spread filling onto the flat side of a cake and top it with another cake. Press gently on top until filling spreads to edges.

Thanksgiving Whoopie Pie

Give thanks to all berries! From wild raspberries to cranberries; from freshly - picked blackberries to carefully chosen red raspberries from the grocery store - celebrate them all! Replace the gooseberries with any of your favorites.

Ingredients

- 2¼ cups flour
- 1 teaspoon baking soda
- 4 oz butter, at room temperature
- 1¼ cups sugar
- 2 eggs
- ½ cup pumpkin puree
- ½ cup gooseberries

Maple Cream

- 8 ounces soft cream cheese
- 1 cup powdered sugar
- 1 tablespoon heavy whipping cream
- 2 tablespoons maple syrup

Makes 20 - 25

Preparation

1. Preheat the oven to 350°F.

2. Line baking sheets with parchment paper or use silicone baking mats.

3. Prepare cakes: In a bowl, using a rubber spatula, mix flour and baking powder.

4. Place butter and sugar in a separate mixing bowl. Beat with the mixer's flat beater, until mixture is light and airy. Then add eggs, one at a time, mixing well.

5. Gradually add dry ingredients (prepared in Step 3), pumpkin puree and gooseberries. Mix until incorporated.

6. Drop batter onto prepared baking sheets, spacing evenly. Spread batter into approximately 1¼-inch circles.

7. Bake for 7-10 minutes or until cakes are springy to the touch and a toothpick, inserted in the center of a cake, comes out clean.

8. Remove from oven and allow to cool completely on a wire rack.

9. Prepare filling: In a separate bowl, mix cream cheese and powdered sugar with the mixer's flat beater, until mixture is light and airy. Add whipping cream and maple syrup (scraping sides of bowl as needed). Mix well until the batter is uniform.

10. When the cakes are completely cool, spread filling onto the flat side of a cake and top it with another cake. Press gently on top until filling spreads to edges.

Happy Birthday Whoopie Cake

Happy Birthday Whoopie Cake

Add color with ½ cup multi-colored sprinkles. On one cake, spread multi-colored sprinkles. This will serve as the upper part or top of the whoopie pie. To ensure that the sprinkles do not fall off, it is important to spread the sprinkles before baking.

Ingredients

- 1¾ cups flour
- 1 teaspoons baking powder
- ½ cup cocoa powder
- 4 oz butter, at room temperature
- 1¼ cups sugar
- Zest of 1 orange
- 1 egg
- 1 cup crème fraiche

French Buttercream Filling

- 4 egg whites
- 1 cup sugar
- 1 teaspoon vanilla extract
- 8 oz butter at room temperature, cut into small cubes

Makes 1 large Whoopie Cake

Preparation

1. Preheat the oven to 350°F. Line baking sheets with parchment paper or use silicone baking mats.

2. Prepare cakes: In a bowl, using a rubber spatula, mix flour, baking powder and cocoa powder.

3. Place butter, sugar and zest of orange in a separate mixing bowl, beating with the mixer's flat beater until mixture is light and airy. Then add the egg, mixing well.

4. Gradually add dry ingredients (prepared in Step 2) and crème fraiche. Mix until incorporated.

5. Drop batter onto prepared baking sheets, spacing evenly. Spread batter into two large circles, approximately 7-8 inches each.

6. Bake for 7-10 minutes or until cakes are springy to the touch and a toothpick, inserted in the center of a cake, comes out clean.

7. Remove from oven and allow to cool completely on a wire rack.

8. Prepare filling: Pour egg whites and sugar into a bowl placed over a pot of hot water (double boiler). Stir constantly until sugar is dissolved.

9. Beat eggs until mixture cools. Then gradually add vanilla extract and butter. Mix until cream is smooth and uniform.

10. When the cakes are completely cool, spread filling onto the flat side of a cake and top it with another cake. Press gently on top until filling spreads to edges.

Winter Chestnut Whoopie Pie

Winter Chestnut Whoopie Pie

This is the perfect Whoopie Pie for a snowy day. To roast the chestnuts, cut a cross in the chestnut and season it as desired. Place the chestnuts in the oven until the cut slot opens up.

Ingredients

- 2 cups flour
- 1½ teaspoons baking powder
- 4 oz butter, at room temperature
- 1¼ cups sugar
- 2 teaspoons vanilla extract or ½ vanilla stick
- 2 eggs
- ½ cup sour cream
- 6 oz chestnut, roasted and peeled, chopped

French Buttercream Filling

- 4 egg whites
- 1 cup sugar
- 1 teaspoon vanilla extract
- 8 oz butter at room temperature, cut into small cubes

Makes 20 - 25

Preparation

1. Preheat the oven to 350°F. Line baking sheets with parchment paper or use silicone baking mats.

2. Prepare cakes: In a bowl, using a rubber spatula, mix flour and baking powder.

3. Place butter, sugar and vanilla extract (or scraped out vanilla beans) in a separate mixing bowl, beating with the mixer's flat beater until mixture is light and airy. Then add eggs, one at a time, mixing well.

4. Gradually add dry ingredients (prepared in Step 2), sour cream and half of the chopped chestnuts. Mix until incorporated.

5. Drop batter onto prepared baking sheets, spacing evenly. Spread batter into approximately 1¼-inch circles.

6. Bake for 7-10 minutes or until cakes are springy to the touch and a toothpick, inserted in the center of a cake, comes out clean.

7. Remove from oven and allow to cool completely on a wire rack.

8. Prepare filling: Pour egg whites and sugar into a bowl placed over a pot of hot water (double boiler). Stir constantly until sugar is dissolved.

9. Beat eggs until mixture cools. Then gradually add vanilla extract and butter. Mix until cream is smooth and uniform. Add the remaining half of the chopped chestnuts into the cream.

10. When the cakes are completely cool, spread filling onto the flat side of a cake and top it with another cake. Press gently on top until filling spreads to edges.

Index

Conversion Charts

The recipes that appear in this cookbook use the standard United States method for measuring liquid and dry or solid ingredients (teaspoons, tablespoons, and cups). The information on this chart is provided to help cooks outside the U.S. successfully use these recipes. All equivalents are approximate.

Useful Equivalents For Cooking/Oven Temperatures

	Fahrenheit	Celsius	Gas Mark
Freeze Water	32° F	0° C	
Room	68° F	20° C	
Temperature	212° F	100° C	
Boil Water	325° F	160° C	3
Bake	350° F	180° C	4
	375° F	190° C	5
	400° F	200° C	6
	425° F	220° C	7
	450° F	230° C	8
Broil			Grill

Metric Equivalents For Different Types Of Ingredients

A standard cup measure of a dry or solid ingredient will vary in weight depending on the type of ingredient. A standard cup of liquid is the same volume for any type of liquid. Use the following chart when converting standard cup measures to grams (weight) or milliliters (volume).

Standard Cup	FinePowder (ex. flour)	Grain (ex.rice)	Granular (ex. sugar)	Liquid Solids (ex. butter)	Liquid (ex. milk)
1	140 g	150 g	190 g	200 g	240 ml
¾	105 g	113 g	143 g	150 g	180 ml
²/₃	93 g	100 g	125 g	133 g	160 ml
½	70 g	75 g	95 g	100 g	120 ml
¹/₃	47 g	50 g	63 g	67 g	80 ml
¼	35 g	38 g	48 g	50 g	60 ml
⅛	18 g	19 g	24 g	25 g	30 ml

Useful Equivalents For Liquid Ingredients By Volume

¼ tsp				1 ml
½ tsp				2 ml
1 tsp	1 tbls		½ fl oz	5 ml
3 tsp	2 tbls	⅛ cup	1 fl oz	15 ml
	4 tbls	¼ cup	2 fl oz	30 ml
	5⅓ tbls	¹/₃ cup	3 fl oz	60 ml
	8 tbls	½ cup	4 fl oz	80 ml
	10²/₃ tbls	²/₃ cup	5 fl oz	120 ml
	12 tbls	¾ cup	6 fl oz	160 ml
	16 tbls	1 cup	8 fl oz	180 ml
	1 pt	2 cups	16 fl oz	240 ml
	1 qt	4 cups	32 fl oz	480 ml
			33 fl oz	960 ml
				1000 ml 1 liter

Useful Equivalents For Dry Ingredients By Weight

(To convert ounces to grams,multiply the number of oz by 30.)			
	1 oz	¹/₁₆ lb	30g
	4 oz	¼ lb	120g
	8 oz	½ lb	240g
	12 oz	¾ lb	480g

Useful Equivalents For Length

(To convert inches to centimeters multiply number of inches by 2.5.)				
	1 in			2.5 cm
	6 in	½ ft		15 cm
	12 in	1 ft		30 cm
	36 in	3 ft	1 yd	90 cm
	40 in			100 cm 1 m